PROPHETIC INSIGHTS FOR DAILY LIVING

VOLUME 1

~~

Inspired Messages From The Holy Spirit

Sheila Eismann

Sheila Eismann

Books by Sheila Eismann

A STORMY YEAR – BOOK 2 OF THE SABBLONTI SERIES

A WOMAN OF SUBSTANCE – A 12-WEEK BIBLE STUDY

CREATIVE AUTHORS' WORKBOOK JOURNAL – A STEP-BY-STEP GUIDE FOR YOUR WRITING EXPERIENCE

HEART TO HEART FROM GOD'S WORD

LOVE, THE TIE THAT BINDS – BOOK 3 OF THE SABBLONTI SERIES

JANTZI'S JOKERS – BOOK 1 OF THE SABBLONTI SERIES

POETRY TIME – VOLUME ONE

PROPHETIC INSIGHTS FOR DAILY LIVING – MESSAGES INSPIRED BY THE HOLY SPIRIT – VOLUME 1

PROPHETIC INSIGHTS FOR DAILY LIVING – MESSAGES INSPIRED BY THE HOLY SPIRIT – VOLUME 2

PROPHETIC INSIGHTS FOR DAILY LIVING – MESSAGES INSPIRED BY THE HOLY SPIRIT – VOLUME 3

RECOGNIZE YOUR CIRCLES

STIRRINGS OF THE SPIRIT

STRAIGHT FROM THE HORSE'S TROUGH

THE CHRISTMAS TIN

Copyright © 2021 by Sheila Eismann.

www.sheilaeismann.com

All rights reserved. No portion of this book may be reproduced, stored in a retrieval system, or transmitted in any form or by any means — electronic, mechanical, photocopy, recording, scanning, or other — except for brief quotations in critical reviews or articles, without the prior written permission of the publisher.

Published by Desert Sage Press
www.desertsagepress.com

Printed and bound in the United States of America.

Cover design by Cathie Richardson. www.countrygardenstitchery.com
All rights reserved.

Any trademarks, service marks, product names, or named features are used only for reference, are assumed to be the property of their respective owners, and the use of any one of those terms does not imply an endorsement on the part of the author and/or the publisher.

ISBN: 978-1-7373135-0-2

Library of Congress Control Number: 2021912322

Scriptures are taken from the New King James Version. Copyright 1979, 1980, 1982 by Thomas Nelson, Inc. Used by permission. All rights reserved.

Scripture quotations marked (NIV) are taken from the Holy Bible, New International Version®, NIV®. Copyright © 1973, 1978, 1984, 2011 by Biblica, Inc.® Used by permission of Zondervan. All rights reserved worldwide. www.zondervan.com. The "NIV" and "New International Version" are trademarks registered in the United States Patent and Trademark Office by Biblica, Inc.®

DEDICATION

This series of workbooks is dedicated to my beloved husband, Dan, who our precious grandkiddos affectionately refer to as "Poppy." He's my best friend, confidant, loyal companion, and fellow believer in our Lord and Savior, Jesus Christ. I will be forever grateful for God knitting our hearts together in His love and giving us compatible and mutually beneficial spiritual giftings.

We've experienced challenges, supreme blessings, miracles, and victories during the 38 years of our marriage. God has sustained us every single day and step of the way by His mighty right hand, His beloved Son, Jesus Christ, The Holy Spirit, His Word, and His ministering angels.

We're eternally grateful for all of the divine appointments God has orchestrated with those of His choosing throughout the intersections of our lives.

It's been the honor and privilege of a lifetime to walk side-by-side with Dan as we continue to learn, laugh, and love together. To God be the glory, both now and forever more!

Sheila Eismann

ACKNOWLEDGEMENTS

My heartfelt gratitude, sincere appreciation, and blessings are extended to Cathie Richardson, Lesta Chadez, and Marilyn Battisti for their invaluable assistance and encouragement in publishing this set of prophetic workbooks.

It's been a special joy to share this experience with my oldest daughter, Cathie, whose artistic gifts and talents bless me beyond measure. For a real treat, please check out her website: **www.countrygardenstitchery.com**

Fifty-three years ago, Lesta and I lived in the same small rural area. Our paths reconnected at just the right time. Despite navigating her own set of life's challenges, Lesta's dynamic combination of mercy and exhortation is a bonus for any writer. In addition, she's a poet, author, and spiritual song writer.

Being a retired school teacher, Marilyn operates from a unique vantage point concerning almost everything she reads and studies, especially as it relates to spiritual matters. I continue to be amazed when reading her thoughts if she opts to post a comment on my website after I've authored one of my blog posts! Since Marilyn has a real heart for intercessory prayer, she's blessed my life immensely as a prayer partner.

In addition, I want to thank my Lord Jesus for helping me every day in every way. With Him, all things are possible. (Matthew 19:26) I'm grateful for The Holy Spirit and His gifts of creativity which are inherent within each of us in various forms.

TABLE OF CONTENTS

Introduction	13
Prophetic Dream # 1 Featuring Silver Coins	27
Prophetic Dream # 2 Featuring Silver Coins	32
Prophetic Vision ~~ The Angel & The Zebra	37
The Stubborn Knot You're Facing	44
"These Are The Days Of The Dramatic!"	51
Angels At The Ports	59
Sunflowers, Sunshine & Shadows	67
The Four Communions	73
The Ox, The Oxbow & The Birdwatcher	80
The Forearm, The Torn Map & The Bird's Nest	88
Cindy, Dean & The Test	96
Two Ladies, Reptiles & Horses	104
A Reed Shaken In The Wind	113
Trapped By The Trappings	120
The Closet, Canoe & Calm	130
The Missing Piece	137
SOL: Spirit of Lawlessness	145
Give Thanks	156
The Hand, The Keys and The Bridge	163
The Frozen Footprint	173
Kindness ~~ An Invaluable Currency	184

Comfort at Christmas	193
Prophetic Dream ~~ Rehashing The Past	202
About The Author	211
Other Books Available from Sheila Eismann, Dan Eismann & Desert Sage Press	213
Notes and Reflections	218

FOREWARD

Woven into the fabric of our lives wherein a silver cord is intertwined throughout the tapestry, there are people in our circle of friends where our hearts are bound together through the Holy Spirit. Sheila Eismann is a special friend that God has placed in my life as the Lord has knit our hearts together in His love. We grew up in the same rural town, and our parents were friends. From this friendship, a bond of love was birthed.

As I have read Sheila's books and followed her writings and blogs over the years, her prophetic visions and dreams have ministered to me in many areas. I give praise to our Lord and Savior Jesus Christ for the many ways He has been with me throughout my life. The Lord especially filled my heart with a living hope through a time of testing when my husband entered into his eternal home in 2019. Special friends like Sheila prayed for me through this difficult journey, and I will be forever grateful for the many ways the Lord has strengthened me and given me hope.

Sheila has a gifting and unique way of weaving in words of wisdom, encouragement, and exhortation as she shares with us what the Lord has given her in visions, dreams, and prophetic words. When we face times of trouble, testing, or tribulation, she has a way of bringing her messages to a practical application in our daily lives by sharing words of comfort and hope while challenging us to pursue a deeper walk with the Lord.

The prophetic visions and dreams the Lord has shared with Sheila are for anyone who wants a fresh infusion of faith and strength to start each day. They are for those walking through difficult seasons of life such as loneliness, grief, or change. The wisdom the Lord shares with her may be for those who are overwhelmed by life's challenges and for those who may be concerned about loved ones or the condition of the world around us. When it seems like the circumstances of life and the storms that surround us are pulling us under, she reminds us that the Lord is the Victor and encourages us to continue to put our trust and hope in Him as He is faithful and true to His promises and His Holy Word.

Every day we need wisdom and fresh insight as we walk out the fullness of our salvation in our journey through this earthly life. The workbooks that Sheila has prepared can be a devotional and also used in a Bible study. Her prophetic writings will be a blessing to those who have open hearts ready to receive what the Lord has for them.

Lesta Chadez, Poet, Spiritual Song Writer, and Author of *Treasures Hidden In Plain Sight, A Collection of Poems and Short Stories.*

You will be ever so blessed to read the prophetic articles by Sheila Eismann. Each of her visions is a timely message to guide and direct you in your everyday living. Having the inspiration from The Holy Spirit, each of Sheila's writings is a direct appointment for you to individually meet with our Lord Jesus and find manna for your soul. Sheila's prophetic visions will definitely inspire you and lift you to another level of Christianity!

Marilyn Battisti, Retired Educator

INTRODUCTION

Prophetic Insights For Daily Living was written with you, the spiritual seeker, Bible reader, and student, in mind to render assistance regarding spiritual gifts, dreams, visions, and prophetic words.

To introduce this new series of workbooks, I deem it's important to go into greater detail concerning the three revelatory gifts of the Holy Spirit listed in 1 Corinthians 12:4-11. These gifts are the word of wisdom, the word of knowledge, and the discerning of spirits.

"There are diversities of gifts, but the same Spirit. There are differences of ministries, but the same Lord. And there are diversities of activities, but it is the same God who works all in all. But the manifestation of the Spirit is given to each one for the profit *of all:* **for to one is given the word of wisdom through the Spirit, to another the word of knowledge through the same Spirit**, to another faith by the same Spirit, to another gifts of healings by the same Spirit, to another the working of miracles, to another prophecy, **to another discerning of spirits**, to another *different* kinds of tongues, to another the interpretation of tongues. But one and the same Spirit works all these things, distributing to each one individually as He wills." [Emphasis mine]

Writing to the church at Corinth, Paul said, "Now concerning spiritual *gifts*, brethren, I do not want you to be ignorant:" [1 Corinthians 12:1]

During its establishment phase, God did not want the church in Corinth to be ignorant concerning these matters, and His desire is no less for present-day churches or Bible-believing Christians.

An important aspect to remember is the Holy Spirit distributes His gifts to each one individually as He wills. [1 Corinthians 12:11] Every single one of the spiritual gifts outlined in 1 Corinthians 12:4-10 is precisely just that, a gift which cannot be bought, traded, manufactured, contrived, manipulated, or you fill in the blank.

<u>The Holy Spirit gift of the word of wisdom and the gift of the word of knowledge:</u>

"Before we begin our study of the gifts of the Holy Spirit, it is important for us to understand that in the scriptures there is a mingling of gifts, so much so that at times we may question just which gift (or gifts) is being manifested. This need cause us no real concern, for it must be remembered that all of the gifts flow from the same source, The Holy Spirit. If we are unable to identify exactly and classify perfectly, let us not be overly concerned. As humans, it is our nature to draw neat lines of separation and classification, but when we seek to impose this practice upon God, we only frustrate ourselves, and we may generate unnecessary confusion.

The word of wisdom and the word of knowledge are two gifts that often work together. Throughout the Old Testament when the prophets would prophesy, the word of wisdom and the word of knowledge would flow together (knowledge, and what to do about it.) In reading the prophetic books of the Old Testament, you will notice the phrase time and time again, "The WORD of the Lord came to _____ (name)." Examples of this can be found in 1 Kings 17:8; Jeremiah 1:4-8; Ezekiel 1:3; Joel 1:1 and Haggai 1:1.

In the New Testament, much of the writings of Paul, Peter, James, and Jude are the word of wisdom and word of knowledge. Also, John's letters to the churches in Revelation chapters 2-3 are this mixture. The word of wisdom often comes with the word of knowledge so that believers in Christ will know how to apply that knowledge correctly. These gifts are two of the three gifts that 'reveal' something. We call these gifts revelation gifts because they consist of information supernaturally revealed from God. Each of these gifts is the God-given ability to receive from Him facts concerning something, anything, about which it is humanly impossible for us to know, revealed to the believer so that he or she may be protected, pray more effectively, or help someone in need.

The gift of the word of knowledge is supernatural in character. It is not obtained by logic, or deduction, reasoning, etc., or by natural senses, but by supernatural revelation through The Holy Spirit. It is the sheer gift of God. It is not essentially a vocal gift. It is received quietly and inaudibly within the person's spirit. It may become vocal when shared with others.

A basic definition of the word of knowledge: a fragment or small item of God's knowledge, supernaturally revealed to a person by The Holy Spirit.

An example of a spoken word of knowledge can be found in John 1:47-49:

'Jesus saw Nathanael coming toward Him, and said of him, 'Behold, an Israelite indeed, in whom is no deceit!'

Nathanael said to Him, 'How do You know me?'

Jesus answered and said to him, 'Before Philip called you, when you were under the fig tree, I saw you.'

Nathanael answered and said to Him, 'Rabbi, You are the Son of God! You are the King of Israel!'

It is important to consider what the word of knowledge is not:

- It is not human knowledge gained by natural means.

- It is not human knowledge sanctified by God.

- It cannot be gained by intellectual learning, studying books, or pursuing academics.

- It is not the ability to study, understand, or interpret the Bible.

- It is not a psychic phenomenon or extra-sensory perception such as telepathy (the supposed ability to be able to read minds), clairvoyance (the supposed ability to know things that are happening elsewhere), or precognition (the supposed ability to know the future.)

The gifts of the Spirit defy human scientific explanation and are not acquired by ordinary educational processes. No amount of education or learning can produce them. They are not dependent upon innate human qualities. For example, the word of wisdom might be spoken by a person of even less than ordinary wisdom. They are not accentuated natural talents and abilities. The least talented or able may as likely be the agent through whom God works as the most intellectually endowed.

It is a subtle ploy of the great deceiver of our souls to attempt to humanize the supernatural and to reduce the spiritual gifts to the level of mere human endowments, talents, and learned or acquired abilities.

A word of knowledge may be revealed to a believer in any of the following ways:

- A sudden inspiration or a deep inner impression.

- A dream, vision, or picture seen through the eye of the spirit, with the interpretation of what is seen.

- Hearing the voice of God, or of angels, audibly or in the ear of the spirit.

- A living personal word from the Lord through scripture.

- The vocal gifts of the Holy Spirit such as tongues, interpretation of tongues or prophecy. [1 Corinthians 12:10]

Supernatural visions and dreams are usually the word of wisdom or word of knowledge in operation. Acts 2:17-18 reminds us of what was spoken by the prophet Joel,

> *'And it shall come to pass in the last days, says God,*
> *That I will pour out of My Spirit on all flesh;*
> *Your sons and your daughters shall prophesy,*
> *Your young men shall see visions,*
> *Your old men shall dream dreams.*
> *And on My menservants and on My maidservants*
> *I will pour out My Spirit in those days;*
> *And they shall prophesy.'*

The word of knowledge may not always be fully understood by the receiver or the hearers. It can seem like it's a riddle or a mystery. In the seventh and eighth chapters of the book of Daniel, we read where the prophet was troubled in his spirit, and the visions that were given to him disturbed him greatly. In Daniel 8:27b, God's servant was appalled by the vision, and it was beyond his understanding.

Oftentimes God will use a word of knowledge to uncover sin, bring people to Him, give guidance and direction, minister encouragement, or impart knowledge of future events. Some Bible scholars teach the revelation of future events to be the gift of the word of wisdom rather than the word of knowledge since wisdom usually pertains to what to do in the future.

If you would like to take the time to examine some examples of a word of knowledge in the Bible, I have listed a few from the Old Testament and the New Testament.

Old Testament:

- 1 Samuel 3:10-14
- 1 Samuel 10:17-23
- 1 Kings 19:11-18
- 2 Kings 5:20-27
- 2 Kings 6:8-23

New Testament:

- Luke 2:25-26

- John 1:29-34
- John 6:60-61
- John 13:38
- Acts 5:1-11

Hosea 4:6a reminds us that God's people are destroyed for lack of knowledge. We definitely need the gift of the word of knowledge operating in our lives and churches today!

The word of wisdom is a flash of inspiration. It is a supernatural revelation sufficient for the occasion of the wisdom or purpose of God. It is the wisdom needed to meet a particular situation, or answer a particular question, or utilize a particular piece of information.

Once again, it is vital to consider what the word of wisdom is and is not:

- It is not natural wisdom.
- It is not the wisdom gained from academic achievement.
- It is not wisdom gained from experience.
- It is not even the wisdom to understand the Bible.
- It is given as the Holy Spirit wills (1 Corinthians 12:11).
- It is given for a specific need or situation.

A word of wisdom may be revealed to a believer in Christ the same way that I have listed previously for the word of knowledge.

It is helpful to know that we can pray for wisdom, understanding, and knowledge. In Ephesians 1:17, Paul prayed for the spirit of wisdom and revelation. In Colossians 1:9, Paul asked God to fill the believers in the church in Colosse with the knowledge of His will in all wisdom and spiritual understanding.

The following are examples of a word of wisdom found in the Old Testament and the New Testament:

Old Testament:

- Genesis 6:13-21

- Genesis 41:33 with Acts 7:10
- Exodus 28:3; 31:6 and 35:26
- Judges 7:5
- 2 Samuel 5:17-25

New Testament:
- Matthew 2:12-15
- Matthew 21:23-27
- Luke 20:22-26
- John 8:3-7
- Acts 27:23-26[i]

The Holy Spirit gift of discerning of spirits:

"The third gift along with the word of wisdom and word of knowledge that reveals something is the gift of discerning of spirits. It has a narrower range than the other two because it is limited to the spirit world.

Sometimes this gift has been called the gift of discernment which is in error. It is the gift of discerning of spirits. It is not the gift of discerning people; it is the gift of discerning of spirits. There is a huge difference.

From our study of scripture, we learn that there are four basic categories of spirits in the spirit world which are as follows:

- God - John 4:24
- Angels – Hebrews 1:14
- Evil spirits, deceiving spirits and demons - Ephesians 6:12; 1 Timothy 4:1 and Revelation 16:14
- Man - Zechariah 12:1; 1 Corinthians 2:11a

A believer in Christ may be (1) operating under the inspiration of the Holy Spirit; or (2) expressing his or her own thoughts, feelings, and desires from his or her soul or spirit; or (3) allowing an alien spirit to oppress him or her and be bringing thoughts from that wrong spirit. An unbeliever in Christ may be completely possessed by an evil spirit. (Luke 8:26-39) The gift of discerning of spirits immediately reveals what is taking place. This gift is given to know what is in a person and to know the spirit that motivates him or her.

First, we need to define the word 'discern.' It is looking beyond the outward to the inward, literally, 'seeing right through', or 'insight.' In the gift of discerning of spirits, it means to distinguish between good and evil spiritual influences.

The following three verses are a sample of how the word 'discern' is used in the Bible:

- 2 Samuel 14:17 – 'And now your servant [the woman from Tekoa] says, 'May the word of my lord the king bring me rest, for my lord the king is like an angel of God in discerning good and evil. May the LORD your God be with you.' [NIV]

- 2 Samuel 19:35a – 'I [Barzillai the Gileadite] *am* today eighty years old. Can I discern between the good and bad?'

- Ezekiel 44:23 – 'And they [the priests] shall teach My people *the difference* between the holy and the unholy, and cause them to discern between the unclean and the clean.'

Some Biblical scholars believe that if there are no visions, (actually **seeing** the spirit), it is not the gift of discerning of spirits, but rather the gift of the word of knowledge in operation. They reason that if one is informed about a spirit, but has no vision of the spirit, he or she would not **discern** it. In some cases, a WORD comes first, then a vision follows.

Through the gift of discerning of spirits, we can discern the origin of certain actions, teachings, and circumstances that have been inspired by spiritual beings. It is the ability given by God to know what spirit is motivating a person or situation. The gift allows a believer to detect and identify spirits and provides supernatural revelation of the unseen spirit world, both good and evil. The real nature of this gift is knowing and judging – never guessing.

The gift of discerning of spirits is not a natural critical spirit, insight into human nature, human shrewdness, character reading, fault-finding, psychological insight, or even spiritual discernment. It is not a spiritual gift to uncover human failings. It is not the spirits of people who have died. It has nothing to do with spiritism or spiritualism. The spirits of departed human beings are not on this earth and to attempt to contact them is forbidden. [Deuteronomy 18:9-12]

Discerning of spirits is needed primarily to reveal the source of spirits. The first and most obvious function of this gift is to reveal the presence of evil spirits in the lives of people or churches. However, it also functions to evaluate the source of a prophetic message, a particular teaching, or some supernatural manifestation. The person functioning with this gift will be able to tell whether the source of the message or act is demonic, divine, or merely human. The gift of discerning of spirits enables a Christian to pick out the source of gifts and messages that truly come from God. Humans cannot be in contact with or understand the spiritual realm except by the power of God or the power of Satan. (1 Corinthians 2:14)

Although the gift has to do primarily with evil spirits, it also is the ability to detect the presence of the Holy Spirit. Visions, seeing Jesus or angels are also included in the discerning of spirits. If one only discerns evil spirits, then the Holy Spirit gift of discerning of spirits is not in operation.

Our natural discernment can be easily fooled. The gift of discerning of spirits is a means of protection from satanic deception. It is easy to confuse the words of the spirit of Satan with those of the Spirit of God. Satan counterfeits the beautiful works of God by creating an outward appearance that is similar to the real work of the Holy Spirit.

Satan is known as the deceiver [Revelation 12:9], the father of lies [John 8:44], and the serpent [Revelation 20:2]. All these titles signify the subtle, crafty deceptiveness which he uses to bring about evil whenever he can. Many times, his counterfeit is so plausible that one will be entirely deceived unless someone is present who functions with the supernatural gift of discerning of spirits. If demon activity was always so obviously reeking with evil and wicked intent, as we tend to imagine, there would no use for this gift of the Holy Spirit."[ii]

The following are examples of discerning of spirits found in the Old Testament and the New Testament:

Old Testament:

- Genesis 21:17-19
- Leviticus 19:31
- Deuteronomy 32:17
- Judges 13:3-7
- 1 Samuel 16:14-15, 23

- 1 Samuel 28:11-19
- 1 Kings 19:5-8
- 2 Kings 6:17
- 2 Chronicles 18:18-22
- Zechariah 3:1-2

New Testament:
- Matthew 1:20-21
- Matthew 16:23
- Luke 1:11-20; 26-38
- Luke 13:11, 16
- Acts 12:7-10
- Acts 13:9-11
- Acts 27:23-24
- 1 John 4:1"

Despite teachings to the contrary, God's people do receive dreams, visions, and prophetic words today. Here's a basic overview of this aspect of the revelatory realm:

1. God communicates through His prophets in one of two ways. "Let the prophet who has a dream tell the dream, but let him who has my word speak my word faithfully."[iii] As an aside, why would God want to stop communicating to us through prophets? Has He stopped speaking? Do people no longer need to hear from Him?

2. *Nābiy' prophet.* One of the ways God communicates to us is through a *nābiy'* prophet. "This word describes one who was raised up by God and, as such, could only proclaim that which the Lord gave him to say. A prophet could not contradict the Law of the Lord or speak from his own mind or heart."[iv] "I [God] will raise up for them a prophet [*nābiy'*] like you [Moses] from among their brothers. And I will put my words in his mouth, and he shall speak to them all that I command him."[v] Jeremiah was a *nābiy'* prophet, and he tried to refrain from giving the word of the LORD because doing so made him "a reproach and derision all day long."[vi] However, he could not refrain from giving the word of God.

> If I say, "I will not mention him,
>   or speak any more in his name,"
> there is in my heart as it were a burning fire
>   shut up in my bones,
> and I am weary with holding it in,
>   and I cannot.[vii]

3. *Hōzeh* prophets. Another way that God communicates to us is through a *hōzeh* or *chōzeh* prophet (hereinafter *hōzeh* prophet). "The word is "[a] masculine noun meaning a seer, prophet. . . . The word means one who sees or perceives; it is used in parallel with the participle of the verb that means literally to see, to perceive. . . . It appears that the participles of *hōzeh* and *rā'āh* function synonymously. But, terminology aside, a seer functioned the same as a prophet, who was moved by God and had divinely given insight."[viii] *Rā'āh* or *rō'eh* is "a verb meaning to see" and can "connote a spiritual observation and comprehension by means of seeing visions."[ix]

A prophet can function as both a *nābiy'* prophet and a *hōzeh* prophet. For example, Jeremiah functioned as both.

> But the LORD said to me,
>   "Do not say, 'I am only a youth';
>   for to all to whom I send you, you shall go,
>   and whatever I command you, you shall speak.
>   . . . .
>   declares the LORD."
> Then the LORD put forth His hand and touched my mouth, and the LORD said to me:
>   "Behold, I have put My words in your mouth.
>   . . . .
>   And the word of the LORD came to me, saying, "Jeremiah, what do you see?" And I said, "I see an almond branch." Then the LORD said to me, "You have seen well, for I am watching over my word to perform it."[x]

King David was assigned all three types of prophets.

Now the acts of King David, from first to last, are written in the Chronicles of Samuel the seer [*rā'āh*], and in the Chronicles of Nathan the prophet [*nābiy'*], and in the Chronicles of Gad the seer [*hōzeh*], with accounts of all his rule and his might and of the circumstances that came upon him and upon Israel and upon all the kingdoms of the countries.[xi]

4. **Examples of the ministry of prophets include the following:**

   a. **Rebuking someone for sin.**

   The L ORD sent Nathan the prophet to David to tell him a story about a rich man who stole and prepared for eating a lamb that had been raised in the home of a poor man.[xii]

   Then David's anger was greatly kindled against the man, and he said to Nathan, "As the L ORD lives, the man who has done this deserves to die, and he shall restore the lamb fourfold, because he did this thing, and because he had no pity."[xiii]

   Nathan then said to David "You are the man!" referring to David having Uriah the Hittite killed in battle in order to cover the sin of David's adultery with Bathsheba.[xiv]

   b. **Turning peoples' hearts to the L ORD.**

   An angel appeared to Zechariah and told him that Elizabeth, his wife who was barren and advanced in years, would have a child, "[a]nd he [John the Baptist] will turn many of the children of Israel to the Lord their God."[xv]

   c. **Bringing people back into a covenant relationship with God.**

   And they abandoned the house of the L ORD, the God of their fathers, and served the Asherim and the idols. And wrath came upon Judah and Jerusalem for this guilt of theirs. Yet he sent prophets among them to bring them back to the L ORD. These testified against them, but they would not pay attention.[xvi]

   d. **Warning of what will occur in the future.**

   Now in these days prophets came down from Jerusalem to Antioch. And one of them named Agabus stood up and foretold by the Spirit that there would be a great famine over all the world (this took place in the days of Claudius). So the disciples determined, everyone according to his ability, to send relief to the brothers living in Judea. And they did so, sending it to the elders by the hand of Barnabas and Saul.[xvii]

   e. **Exhorting and strengthening the brethren.**

And Judas and Silas, who were themselves prophets, encouraged and strengthened the brothers with many words.[xviii]

f. Giving divine direction.

Now there were in the church at Antioch prophets and teachers, Barnabas, Simeon who was called Niger, Lucius of Cyrene, Manaen a lifelong friend of Herod the tetrarch, and Saul. While they were worshiping the Lord and fasting, the Holy Spirit said, "Set apart for me Barnabas and Saul for the work to which I have called them." Then after fasting and praying they laid their hands on them and sent them off.[xix]

g. Speaking against sin; warning of judgment, and preaching about hope and renewal.

Then the Lord put out his hand and touched my mouth. And the Lord said to me,
> "Behold, I have put my words in your mouth.
> See, I have set you this day over nations and over kingdoms,
> to pluck up and to break down,
> to destroy and to overthrow,
> to build and to plant."[xx]

Jeremiah's message is threefold: (1) he must **pluck up** and **break down**, which refers to preaching against sin; (2) he must **destroy** and **overthrow**, which relates to messages concerning judgment; and (3) he must **build** and **plant**, which means he must preach about hope and renewal."[xxi]

All prophets do not have the same anointing or spiritual assignments. Some are called to prophesy to the people, some to persons in government, some to individuals, and some to geographic regions, mountains, land, rivers, etc. In addition, some receive prophecies more frequently than others. "Do not despise prophecies, but test everything; hold fast what is good."[xxii]

We are not to blindly accept what is prophesied. In church, "[l]et two or three prophets speak and let the others weigh what is said. If a revelation is made to another sitting there, let the first be silent. For you can all prophesy one by one, so that all may learn and all be encouraged, and the spirits of prophets are subject to prophets."[xxiii] A prophet may be male or female.[xxiv]

My personal prayer is that you will be enlightened, strengthened, and encouraged as you study this workbook and record what God, Jesus, and The Holy Spirit reveal to you. Time spent with Them along with reading and studying the Bible yields great dividends.

Please check out my new website: **www.sheilaeismann.com**

Also, if you would like to send an email or have questions about this workbook, my address is **sheila@sheilaeismann.com**. Thank you!

"The LORD bless you and keep you;
 The LORD make His face shine upon you,
 And be gracious to you;
 The LORD lift up His countenance upon you,
 And give you peace." (Numbers 6:24-26)

Sheila Eismann

Prophetic Dream #1 Featuring Silver Coins

August 13, 2020
Prophetic Dreams

During the night of August 6th, 2020, I received the first of two prophetic dreams. In this blog post, I will be writing about prophetic dream #1 featuring silver coins.

In the first dream, I needed to pay for some type of project our local grandchildren were doing at their school which required $1.50 in change. I looked inside a box and searched underneath a leather purse.

First, I saw a couple of old silver dollars. Suddenly, these dollars supernaturally expanded to look like new, brilliant, silver eagle dollars which were 5 inches in diameter. Obviously, this could not happen in real life, but this is how they appeared in the dream.

As I continued to sift through the contents of the box, I located a few other coins and was able to count out exactly one (silver) dollar and 50 cents, so I tendered the exact amount for the school project.

End of dream.

Some thoughts and/or symbolism regarding this dream:

Silver = knowledge and redemption (John 17:3)
Silver coins = revelation knowledge (Proverbs 2:3-4)

In this dream, I had to look and search for these coins. We must look and search for revelation knowledge for whatever situation is needed which in this case pertained to our grandchildren's school project.

The expansion of the size of the coins from their original size to the 5 inches in diameter meant they should be more valuable because of increased silver content. The coins became shiny after they increased in size. Silver tarnishes, so this shows they are related to the present time rather than the past. But the expanded coin didn't purchase any more than the old coin. It only paid for what was previously a $1.00 item. Therefore, and with the increased silver in the expanded coin, it should have been more valuable. The new, expanded coin was not worth any more than the old coin.

With the silver coins expanding so rapidly with new silver content to add to their brilliance, it could signal sudden, hyperinflation. If this is the case, a dollar would still be worth only a dollar. With inflation, there are more dollars in circulation, but they do not have increased purchasing power. It takes more dollars to purchase the same goods. The larger dollars (5 inches in diameter) would take more money to purchase the same thing. The increased size should increase the value of the coin, but it did not because it could only purchase what could have been purchased with the smaller coin. If inflation is coming, what are you doing to prepare?

Listed below are some additional symbolisms from the dream:

Five (the new silver coins expanded to 5 inches in diameter) = God's gift to man and man's responsibility; works, and service.
Grandchildren = Our natural and spiritual legacies.
Purse = Treasure, heart, precious, valuable. (Matthew 6:21)

As I continue to intercede for our grandchildren and other school students, my prayer is that knowledge and strategies would come to teachers and administrators for the upcoming school year as they search all possibilities (in the dream, I searched for the other coins.) In addition, the knowledge and new strategies would come "suddenly" for teachers and "greatly expand" as the silver dollars did in the dream.

With the overall theme of silver, I'm praying that the time is redeemed with "brilliance" and "newness" (the beautiful, new silver coins) for the loss of a portion of the last school year as it's folded into a new school year.

This would apply to however the child(ren) were being educated whether it be at home, online, in the public, private, or charter schools, etc.

Prophetic Insights for Daily Living:

How have you been led to pray for the schools in your area?
_____
_____
_____
_____

1. Perhaps you have been given some strategy to share with teachers and/or school personnel from which everyone would benefit.
2. Are you willing to look around, dig through what you have, and donate toward the continued education of our children and grandchildren?
_____

3. Have you or the geographic region in which you are living experienced any hyperinflation? If so, what has been the most dramatic increase?
_____
_____
_____

4. There is a confirmation to the dream which I received on August 26, 2020, which is posted online on June 10, 2021. You can copy and paste the link below into your browser if you would like to read it.

https://www.npr.org/2021/06/10/1004806688/inflation-is-surging-the-price-of-a-toyota-pickup-truck-helps-explain-why

I will post the second prophetic dream in a separate blog post.

https://sheilaeismann.com/prophetic-dream-2-featuring-silver-coins/
Sending many blessings to you and your family, and please continue to pray for students and their upcoming school year.

Sheila Eismann, Prophetic Seer, Blogger, Author & Teacher, publishes her weekly blog posts endeavoring to encourage others through God's word. Her writings include teaching and instructions on how to apply prophetic insights for daily living. You can subscribe to receive new blog posts on her website at www.sheilaeismann.com.

Prophetic Dream #2 Featuring Silver Coins

August 13, 2020
Prophetic Dreams

I was given back-to-back prophetic dreams featuring silver coins. The first prophetic dream was given to me during the night of August 6th, 2020, and prophetic dream #2 featuring silver coins followed the next night, August 7th, 2020.

https://sheilaeismann.com/prophetic-dream-1-featuring-silver-coins/

Rarely do I ever receive back-to-back dreams, especially with the same subject matter.

In the second dream, some coins were given to me by a prophetic intercessor friend who's done a lot of spiritual work on behalf of the land, rivers, mountains, and geography within our state.

End of dream.

Even though this dream was extremely short, the repetition of dreams is for emphasis. An example of this would be the two dreams given to Pharaoh in the 41st chapter of Genesis where you can read all about it! Granted, my prophetic dream #2 featuring silver coins doesn't have nearly the magnitude that Pharoah's did, but I'm going to pay close attention and pray into it. The silver coins in this dream were older which would indicate history, knowledge, and background which is really in my P.I.F's (prophetic intercessor friend's) "wheelhouse." This has been part of her destiny and her spiritual assignments covering several decades.

She has diligently labored on behalf of our state spiritually by renaming various landmarks and dedicating them to the kingdom of God and His purposes on earth. She's spent an inordinate amount of time, money, energy, and effort completing her assignments.

Since these coins were a gift to me, I'm still pondering what exactly it is that I'm assigned to do, especially as it relates to our great state.

Practical applications from this dream:

1.That we would visibly see the fruits within our state of my prophetic intercessor friend's efforts from the prior decades. With some of her assignments, other people assisted her as well.

2. When studying the history of our state, I discovered that the territorial boundaries were changed 6 times. Some have opined, "We got the leftovers." Since I was born and raised here, I don't look at it in this manner. Since each state has a destiny, I look forward to witnessing "a first fruits" coming forth from our state.

Biblical examples of geographic spiritual assignments:

Ezekiel 36:1-15 (mountains, hills, rivers, and valleys)

2 Kings 2:19-22 (the water and the land)

Prophetic Insights for Daily Living:

I would like to hear from you as to how you've been led to pray concerning your state and/or the specific needs and spiritual assignments therein.

1. Have you been given any revelation knowledge (silver is symbolic of revelation knowledge – Proverbs 2:3-4) as to the destiny of your state and whether or not it's been fulfilled?

_____
_____
_____
_____

2. Considering your spiritual assignments and God-given destiny, are there people with whom you need to connect to receive revelation knowledge from, so you can complete your assignments?

_____
_____
_____
_____

3. Have you received prophetic dreams in the past? If so, how have they impacted your life or the lives of others?

_____
_____
_____
_____

Many blessings to you and your family. Please continue to pray. (1st Thess. 5:17)

Sheila Eismann, Prophetic Seer, Blogger, Author & Teacher, publishes her weekly blog posts endeavoring to encourage others through God's word. Her writings include teaching and instructions on how to apply prophetic insights for daily living. You can subscribe to receive new blog posts on her website at www.sheilaeismann.com.

Prophetic Vision: The Angel & The Zebra

August 19, 2020
Prophetic Visions

Quoting our youngest granddaughter, "The animal kingdom is "ginormous!" To that end, what is your favorite one if you can limit it to just that? Mine is the horse, of course. Do any of you keep a zebra in your backyard? Let's explore this prophetic vision: The Angel & The Zebra, shall we?

Jeremiah 1:11-13 reads, "Moreover the word of the Lord came to me [Jeremiah], saying, Jeremiah, what do you see?'

And I said, 'I see a branch of an almond tree.'

Then the LORD said to me, 'You have seen well, for I am ready to perform My word.'

And the word of the LORD came to me the second time, saying, 'What do you see?'

And I said, 'I see a boiling pot, and it is facing away from the north.' "

The first vision pertained to an almond tree that blossoms when other trees are dormant. God was watching over this tree and allowed Jeremiah to see it in the unseen spirit realm.

In the second vision, Jeremiah saw a boiling pot facing away from the north, so its contents would have been spilled to the south. This vision was ultimately fulfilled via an attack on Judah and Jerusalem by Babylon from the north.

Ephesians 4:11-16 tells us, "And He Himself [Jesus] gave some to be apostles, some prophets, some evangelists, and some pastors and teachers, for the equipping of the saints for the work of the ministry, for the edifying of the body of Christ, til we all come to the unity of the faith and of the knowledge of the Son of God, to a perfect man, to the measure of the stature of the fullness of Christ; that we should no longer be children, tossed to and fro and carried about with every wind of doctrine, by the trickery of men, in the cunning craftiness of deceitful plotting, but, speaking the truth in love, may grow up in all things into Him who is the head — Christ — from whom the whole body joined and knit together by what every joint supplies, according to the effective working by which every part does its share, causes growth for the edifying of itself in love."

There are basically two categories of prophets: *nabiy* and *hozeh* or *ra'ah*. The Nabiy prophets experience sort of a "bubbling up" from within where they begin to declare the word of the Lord deep from within their spirit. The ra'ah or hozeh prophets typically receive dreams and visions rather than hearing or experiencing audible words. Suddenly, The Holy Spirit of God opens up the Spirit realm to show them mental pictures, dreams, visions, good and/or fallen angels, etc. Some seers are allowed glimpses into the unseen realms. We see an example of this with the prophet Elisha in 2 Kings 6:17.

The primary ministry of a prophet is to help keep people in a covenant relationship with God. [2 Chronicles 24:19] To that end, there are many dimensions of the prophetic realm such as nabiy and ra'ah prophets, prophetic minstrels, dreams, visions, prophecy, words of knowledge, words of wisdom, prophetic song, prophetic dance, etc. Each of these can bring exhortation, edification, comfort, rebuke, correction, give divine direction, speak against sin, warn of judgment, preach about hope and renewal, and on rolls the prophetic river. When a personal prophecy is given, the majority of the time it will confirm what the Lord has already been speaking to the individual or showing him or her.

With this backdrop, I was preparing dinner late Friday evening, August 14th, 2020. Suddenly, a vision opened up in the Spirit realm wherein I saw a zebra standing in the backyard of a close friend and sister in our Lord Jesus Christ. It was facing west at the time.

Since my friend does not live in a zoo or on the continent of Africa, I was quite startled to see this beautiful animal standing there! A few minutes later, the vision expanded to where I saw an angel holding the reins of the bridle which had been placed on the zebra.

Back to the animal kingdom for a moment, if your favorite happens to the zebra, I apologize in advance as this blog post is nothing against that species!

I thought this a bit odd as I'd not remembered ever seeing a zebra in the spirit until this particular evening.

I've had a close relationship for years with the woman in whose backyard the zebra was standing. She asks me to pray for her and her family periodically. During my prayer time later that evening, I asked the Lord if He wanted me to "sit on this vision" and continue to pray into the same or to release it. Quite often, the Lord will use traffic lights to signal to me what He wants me to do with the dreams, visions, and prophetic words He has entrusted to me. I saw a green light, so I knew I must convey the message.

Before doing so, I consulted one of the Biblical symbolism books I have in my prophetic library. I was surprised to learn that the symbolism for zebra is listed as double-mindedness (black and white), lukewarm, and in or about the world. Well, you probably already know I was dreading this phone call!

Due to what I call the "Corona Crud," I've been limiting personal visits even with wearing a mask and social distancing.

Immediately, the church of Laodicea, or "The Lukewarm Church" as it's often called, was quickened unto me. Jesus told the members of this church to be zealous and repent. You can read all about it in Revelation 3:14-22!

When I explained the symbolism and the correlation to one of the 7 churches in the book of Revelation, my sister in the Lord graciously received the input. Unbeknownst to me, she'd been asking the Lord to expose her "blind spots," so she could be holy before Him. I don't think she expected the spots to be stripes, so to speak! At her suggestion and with her permission, I wrote this blog post as my friend desires that her life be a living example to others. Scripture tells us that we are to continue to work on our God-like character with the help of The Holy Spirit. [1st Peter 1:15-16; Leviticus 11:44-45]

The zebra could have appeared anywhere, but in the vision, it was in her backyard. The symbolism equates to that which is private in one's own life; matters concerning you or your own family; past issues; something hidden.

This is not about trying to be perfect as only Jesus was perfect. That's why He could be the propitiation for our sins when He hung on the cross. He defeated death, hell, and the grave, and is now seated at the right hand of the Father in heaven.

Sanctification is an ongoing work of The Holy Spirit. Thankfully, He doesn't require or ask us to deal with everything in our lives simultaneously as that would be overwhelming! He's gracious, but when He quickens something unto us and begins to bring pressure to bear that it's time to deal with it in accordance with His help, it's best to work with Him and not resist.

Just like the stripes on the zebras in real life are individual with no two being the same, we can apply the same thing to ourselves. The spiritual and physical challenges I'm required to address and work on may not necessarily be the same ones you're facing.

Prophetic Insights for Daily Living:

1.If you don't already have an accountability partner or group, I would encourage you to find a trustworthy one. The key word here is trustworthy. Nothing drains our faith account more than when and where confidences are breached. God's word has a lot to say about gossips and talebearers. [Proverbs 16:28; 17:9]

2. This begs the question of how will we know when the angel leads the donkey from my friend's backyard? God never starts something without completing it, so I'm sure The Holy Spirit will let us know.

3. Has there been a time in your life when you've needed to give a challenging message to someone? How did you handle it, and what was the outcome?

_____
_____
_____
_____

Thanks for reading, and many blessings to you and your family!

Sheila Eismann, Prophetic Seer, Blogger, Author & Teacher, publishes her weekly blog posts endeavoring to encourage others through God's word. Her writings include teaching and instructions on how to apply prophetic insights for daily living. You can subscribe to receive new blog posts on her website at www.sheilaeismann.com.

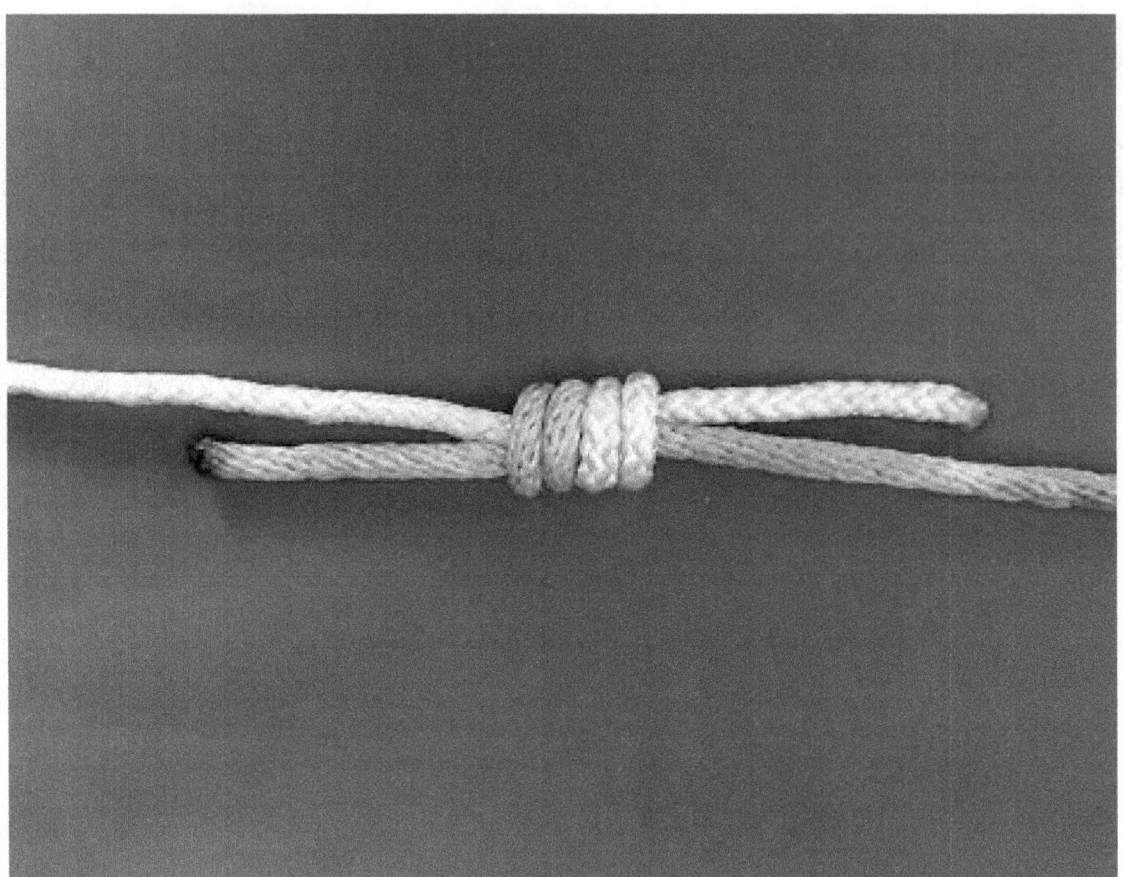

The Stubborn Knot You're Facing
August 26, 2020
Encouragement

Are any of you rock climbers, like to fish, or work for search and rescue? Even if your answer is, "No," you may still be able to identify with this week's prophetic blog post which parallels life's challenges & the stubborn knot you're facing.

The featured photo showcases what's known as a *Double Fisherman's Knot, Grapevine Knot, or Double Englishman's Knot*. These are typically formed by tying together thin, stiff, or slick, ropes or lines to use in instances mentioned in my first paragraph. The main idea behind these types of knots is that they are either impossible or extremely difficult to untie.

I deem there can be categories of stubborn knots. Granted, it may take some time, effort, discovery, and perseverance to discover which one applies whereas some of you readers may already know which one tops your list!

On the other hand, maybe you don't have any. Great! You can go back to cooking dinner or changing the oil in your car or whatever is on your *To-Do List* for today.

Here's somewhat of a practical application if needed:

1. Make a list of your knots (challenges or circumstances).

_____
_____
_____
_____

2. How have you attacked them or what strategies have you used to untie the knots?

_____
_____
_____
_____

3. Have you consulted other people, professionals, resources, etc. to assist you?

_____

4. More importantly, have you taken a deep dive into God's word to sustain you through the process?

From my own life, I have a couple of instances to illustrate my point. During the early years of our marriage, I had been gifted a couple of short, thin necklaces. One of them always seemed to end up in several rigid knots despite my having tried to store it properly after each use. My patient husband would finally get these untied after several attempts. The key word here is patient!

A more recent example would be one wherein I needed to learn a new software program. Since technological areas have never really been my natural strength or in my wheelhouse, I almost thinned all the hair on top of my head trying to figure it out. It's a good thing I have thick hair! I was determined to learn this program and just kept chipping away at it. I finally conquered it, and when I looked into the mirror, I had no bald spots.

Fourteen years ago, I developed cylindrical fascial distortion in which the fascia broke behind my right thigh for no apparent reason. There's no surgical cure for this, and it could not have broken in a more inconvenient spot. Fascia is the connective tissue that holds our muscles, bones, organs, nerve fibers, and blood vessels in place. When I look at a picture of it, I'm reminded of the string used for tennis rackets. It would take a two-volume series of explanations to list what I've tried to conquer this knot to no avail. It's a reversal of sorts as the impossible knots I needed to stay tied within my body ended up untied in spots.

https://www.runnersworld.com/advanced/a20784481/understanding-your-fascia/

Perhaps some of you can relate to the last example if you have an ongoing health issue. Maybe you've lost a loved one or are facing some other insurmountable challenge.

The Apostle Paul comes to mind in this regard. In the 12th chapter of 2nd Corinthians, he speaks of pleading with the Lord to have his thorn in the flesh removed. In these verses, a thorn is the Greek word *skolops* [Strong's G4647] meaning something which causes severe pain or constant irritation, bodily ailment, or infirmity.

It's quite possible Paul's challenge manifested as a physical issue based upon Galatians 4:15, "What then was the blessing you enjoyed? For I bear witness that, if possible, you would have plucked out your own eyes and given them to me." Also, Galatians 6:11, "See with what large letters I have written to you with my own hand!"

Even though the Apostle Paul penned approximately 2/3rds of the New Testament, his life was certainly no picnic or a walk in the park. He experienced shipwrecks, beatings, persecutions, reproaches, lack of physical provision, and imprisonment.

Prophetically speaking, a knot can be symbolic of some type of stronghold such as the spirit of bondage in someone's life which keeps them trapped in a destructive cycle.

Another prophetic symbol would be an enigma such as in Daniel 5:16 when the Prophet Daniel was brought before King Belshazzar to give the interpretation of the writing on the palace wall.

The king said, "And I have heard of you, that you can give interpretations and explain enigmas." One of the words related to enigma is knot [tied up]. Perhaps you have a life-long enigma or riddle you are trying to solve.

Reflection and introspection, guided by The Holy Spirit and God's word, can be of supreme assistance. Some things I've gleaned during my battles with the knots are:

1. It takes God's ongoing strength as we lean into Him daily to keep us strong during these challenges.
2. The spiritual progression of Romans 5:3-5 begins to take shape in our inner man as tribulation produces perseverance, and perseverance, character; and character, hope.
3. The knots force us to choose as to whether or not we will still love and serve God even in difficult times.
4. Our prayer life is solidified through the process and keeps us walking closely with God. Sometimes human nature is such that if everything in our lives in sailing right along peacefully, we can start to drift saying, "Thanks God, I can take it from here." How would you rate your prayer life?

_____

_____

5. They can help to make us more compassionate, loving, and caring people.

6. We learn it's better to cast our cares upon the Lord rather than trying to carry them ourselves as we were never meant to do so. (1st Peter 5:7) If we feel that heaviness from our burdens, we are trying to do the Holy Spirit's job.

Prophetic Insights for Daily Living:

How did you battle discouragement in the process during the time of your life's challenges?

_____
_____
_____

For the "knots" you were able to get untied, how did you persevere until you gained the victory?

_____
_____
_____

What steps or approaches did you implement?

_____
_____
_____

Pertaining to the type you're still battling, what words of advice and encouragement could you render to others?

_____
_____
_____

Not all knots are equal! With the ultra-difficult ones, sometimes we have to let go, and let God.

May the Lord direct your hearts into God's love and Christ's perseverance. (2 Thessalonians 3:5 – NIV) Have a blessed week as you stay safe and strong.

Sheila Eismann, Prophetic Seer, Blogger, Author & Teacher, publishes her weekly blog posts endeavoring to encourage others through God's word. Her writings include teaching and instructions on how to apply prophetic insights for daily living. You can subscribe to receive new blog posts on her website at www.sheilaeismann.com.

"These Are The Days Of The Dramatic!"
August 28, 2020
Prophetic Visions

Upon awakening early August 25, 2020, I heard the following in the Spirit, "These are the days of the dramatic!" The last thing I expected to receive on this hot, summer morning was an angelic message.

I saw an angel with glistening blonde, shoulder-length hair. He was dressed in a white robe while blowing a long, thin, gold trumpet which was about 4 feet long. When he blew the trumpet, a gold piece of paper fell from the end of it. Written on it with red ink were the words, **"Watch for it!"** These specific things were dropped into my spirit:

Beginnings

Deliverances

Discoveries

Endings

Expansions

Healings

Illuminations

Institutions

Invitations

Opportunities

Overthrows

Reconciliations

Reductions

Reversals

Rulings

Salvations

Sights

Sounds

Suddenlies

Ecclesiastes 3:1-8 was quickened unto me which speaks of there is an appointed time for everything under heaven.

https://sheilaeismann.com/spiritual-time/

The above-listed order of things to watch for was not exactly the same in which I heard them in the Spirit; however, I felt led to alphabetize them, so I could enter a page for each one in my prophetic journal for this next season. This will make it easier to enter the confirmations or fulfillments on each page as the dramatic event(s) unfold.

When looking at the categories or words which were given to me, they can seem common or generic. The key word to watch for is ***dramatic***. For instance, some of us can receive invitations or opportunities each week or month, but would they be considered of a dramatic nature?

Some synonyms for dramatic are:

breathtaking
climactic
electrifying
sensational
startling
suddenly
suspenseful
vivid

These events may occur in our individual lives, those of our family members, in our communities, states, nation, or around the globe.

The Bible is replete with dramatic events and suddenlies.

2nd Chronicles Chapter 29 chronicles Hezekiah's kingship and institution of cleansing the temple and restoring worship therein. Verse 36 reads, "Then Hezekiah and all the people rejoiced that God had prepared the people since the events took place so suddenly."

Acts 2:1-2, "When the Day of Pentecost had fully come, they were all with one accord in one place. And suddenly there came a sound from heaven, as of a rushing mighty wind, and it filled the whole house where they were sitting."

In the next scene of the vision on the morning of August 25th, I saw dark-haired, robed angels inside community parks cooking pancakes. While standing in front of their grills, they seemed serious and quite intent on their tasks at hand, especially when flipping the pancakes from one side to the other.

There could well be a play on the word ***flipping*** (the pancakes). In the upcoming days of the dramatic, watch for many things to be flipped, particularly in the above-mentioned categories. Things are going to be flipped suddenly and dramatically.

Cooking pancakes in a city or community park reminded me of the "Pancake Breakfasts" which would be the kick-off event for annual rodeos and other civic events in our geographic region. It would be a time when farmers, ranchers, city folk, and those visiting from other regions could gather to visit and "bat the breeze" as my daddy used to say. These events drew communities together to continue to strengthen the bonds within. Unfortunately, the majority of these annual events have been canceled this year due to the pandemic; however, angelic assistance is being dispatched to communities throughout our country at this time.

Pancakes can be symbolic of love, belonging (to a family or a community), or hospitality. In 1st Kings 17:8-16, we read of the account of Elijah being sent to the widow of Zarephath. Verse 13 states, "And Elijah said to her (the widow), 'Do not fear; go and do as you have said, but make me a small cake from it first, and bring it to me; and afterward make some for yourself and your son.'"

In this verse, the small cake means a disc or cake of bread. It is the Hebrew word *uggah* [Strong's H5692].

I deem there's a prophetic emphasis on the fact that the Prophet Elijah counseled the widow to have no fear even amid lack. In the upcoming days of the ultra-dramatic, we are not to operate in fear. The only fear we are to have is the holy, reverential fear and awe of God. (Job 28:28)

Call to action:

Take your place as a watchman on the wall or at the city gate to continue to pray and intercede for our communities and our nation. (2nd Samuel 10:12; 1st Chronicles 19:13)

I encourage you to have a sense of expectancy regarding dramatic events unfolding. Some of these are going to be negative while some will be positive. Also, some of the negatives will be positives if we can look at them in that manner.

Prophetic Insights for Daily Living:

1. If you're not already doing so, this would be a wonderful time to start prophetic journaling. You can use any type of journal, notebook, theme book, laptop, dictate into the "Notes" section of your smartphone, or whatever is easiest for you.

2. Press in to hear what the Lord is saying to you personally. All of us can hear from Him as Jesus assured us in John 10:27, "My sheep hear My voice, and I know them, and they follow Me." You may not hear an audible voice, but God speaks through His word as you read it or you may have a stirring within your spirit. This is quite often how His will is revealed to us.

3. When you receive what God has downloaded into your spirit commensurate with His will, begin to prophetically declare and decree the word of the Lord. An example of this can be found in Acts 27:21-44.

4. Print off this blog post which lists the specific categories to monitor and listen to or watch for when the angel sounds the trumpet. With the never-ending news cycle each day, it shouldn't be too difficult to ascertain some of them. Record what you see and hear. Also, make note of the date and time.

Regarding the angels which I saw in this vision, they obviously didn't look like the one in the photo featured with this blog post as I wanted to try to locate an image with an elongated golden trumpet.

In my book titled *Stirrings of The Spirit*, I explain additional encounters with angels who have different assignments and give physical descriptions of them. Each one may have a different angelic message.

https://sheilaeismann.com/product/stirrings-of-the-spirit/

Be encouraged in the Lord and in the power of His might. He is the blessed controller of all things. I am encouraging you to stay watchful and remain strong and hopeful. Keep your ears tuned for an angelic message!

Sheila Eismann, Prophetic Seer, Blogger, Author & Teacher, publishes her weekly blog posts endeavoring to encourage others through God's word. Her writings include teaching and instructions on how to apply prophetic insights for daily living. You can subscribe to receive new blog posts on her website at www.sheilaeismann.com.

This workbook is being published almost a year after this prophetic vision was given to me. What dramatic headlines, happenings, circumstances, etc. have you witnessed or read since that time?

Angels at the Ports

September 2, 2020
Prophetic Visions

I awakened at 3:40 a.m., September 1st, 2020, to the words, "Angels at the ports." Angelic activity occurs around us all of the time.

Suddenly, I saw angels standing in a port city overlooking the water.

As I was drawn closer in the spirit realm, I observed that the angels' eyes became binoculars which provided the ability to see long distances and deep under water.

This could mean that the angels were looking long distances away at whatever they were watching which could include something under the water such as submarines. It may mean there's something that's not good which is approaching otherwise they probably wouldn't be assigned or sent there.

In the next scene of the vision, I saw watchmen whose eyes also became supernatural binoculars. It was as if their regular eyes were replaced with these high-powered, heavenly issued (HI) binoculars.

Both the angels' and watchmens' eyes became binoculars that could supernaturally dart back and forth above and under water with ultra, high-powered vision. Angels will partner with the watchmen in these endeavors.

God gives the angels their specific assignments. An example of this would be the angel over the waters referenced in Revelation 16:5. Acts 12:5-7 chronicles the account of the angel helping to free the Apostle Peter from prison.

https://sheilaeismann.com/angelic-message/

The Hebrew words for watchman are:

https://www.blueletterbible.org/lang/Lexicon/Lexicon.cfm?strongs=H6822&t=KJV

Shamar (Strong's H8104) means to keep, guard, observe, give heed.

Tsaphah (Strong's H6822) the meaning of which is to look out or about, spy, keep watch, observe, watch.

Binoculars are symbolic of insight; understanding; spiritual vision; focusing; prophetic vision; faith to be able to see something which couldn't normally be seen with the natural eye; the foreseeable future; expectancy; or a future event.

I heard the word *fort* and knew by revelation that the angels were going to be stationed in supernatural forts down by the waterfronts in the port cities.

This phraseology appeared next, **"The ports need to become forts."** As you read this and ponder angelic activity, what do you think this means? Here's space for you to record your thoughts and insights:

_____
_____
_____
_____
_____
_____
_____
_____
_____

In the next scene of the vision, I saw where the angels were issued royal blue, metal trunks with camel-colored, leather handles on the sides of them to store their belongings. Trunks like these were used in earlier decades in our country when some college students would leave at the end of each summer to head back to school. They would pack their belongings in them if they traveled by car or train. If angels need these trunks, it could indicate they might be in the ports for a while.

Medium or dark blue is symbolic of God's spirit or word.

The words, "Elohim, Adonai" were quickened unto me which are names for God. Elohim designates the one, true God and conveys Creator, King, Judge, Lord, Savior; His faithful character, and He is faithful to His covenant with those who believe in Him. Adonai is used exclusively of God and points to the supreme authority or power of God.

The Biblical verse which reinforces Elohim and Adonai with watchmen is Psalm 127:1b, "Unless the LORD guards the city, the watchman stays awake in vain." These angels have been assigned to be watchmen for the port cities. The earthly watchmen get to partner with the angelic watchmen.

Also, the name "Herman" was dropped into my spirit. When consulting the meaning of the name, I found the following:

"Literal Meaning: 'Army-Man Warrior' – Old German

Suggested Character Quality: Man of Diligence

Suggested Lifetime Scripture Verse: Isaiah 12:2, 'Behold, God is my salvation; I will trust and not be afraid, for Jehovah, the Lord, is my strength and my song. He has become my salvation.'"

Following the release of last week's blog post titled *These Are The Days of The Dramatic!*, I heard from some of you who have subscribed via email to receive weekly blog updates. You indicated that you'd written down the various categories mentioned in the blog post, so you could start monitoring fulfillments thereof.

Two new categories were downloaded into my spirit on Friday, August 29th, so I added them to my master list: **Rescues** and **Trades**.

Perhaps this week's blog post is connected as there may be dramatic rescues at a port or something about a trade of some sort. There will be greater scrutiny regarding trades in the days ahead. Some ports are so busy that there's a tremendous amount of activity within 24 hours; however, nothing gets past the Spirit of God.

The angels are watchmen in the fort at the port. One way in which forts were used during the establishment and settling of our country was to protect ports on the coasts from enemy ships entering the harbors which also protected ships inside the harbors.

Prophetic Insights for Daily Living:

1. This would be a wonderful teaching and mentoring opportunity for older prophets, prophetesses, intercessors, and ministry teams to include younger people. It lends itself to a very practical, interactive, training wherein they could be shown how to look for prophetic signs and learn to pray and prophesy on location.

2. For those of you who have a shofar, plan to blow it, and watch what happens when you do! This releases a significant sound into the atmosphere. This would be an example of a "Prophetic Act." (An example of a prophetic act is Nehemiah 5:13). Do you own a shofar, and have you blown it in a public setting or gathering?

_____
_____
_____

3. Record what you see and hear when you visit the port. Also, this would be an example of a "Prophetic Act."

4. Prophetically declare and decree what you are sensing in the spirit realm which will benefit the ports, cities, and people.

5. An example from scripture for the watchman declaring what he sees can be found in Isaiah 21:6, "For thus has the Lord said to me (Isaiah): 'Go, set a watchman, Let him declare what he sees."

6. How has your spirit been stirred after reading this blog post, and what do you feel led to do?

_____
_____
_____
_____

Prayer Points:

A. This is a clarion call to ramp up the prayers for our nation's ports of which there are many, but it's a definite directive for those who live in or near these places.

B. Sondra, a dear sister in our Lord Jesus Christ and intercessor for our state, was quickened unto me. I've already notified her of this assignment. Even if it's a small port, the activities therein still affect your geographic region, if not the entire globe.

C. Pray for integrity for those who work in this industry and for their safety.

D. Part of the assignment is to watch for harmful cargo entering or leaving our ports and pray accordingly as you are led by The Holy Spirit of God. The ports must be protected just like our land borders.

E. Ports have a ripple effect in our nation, no pun intended.

I can still hear my daddy's booming voice all those years ago when I participated in big game hunts with him. When we would head out early thirty each morning of the adventure, he would command, "Keep your eyes peeled!"

My prayer is that you will remain strong, steadfast, watchful, and always hopeful in our Lord Jesus Christ. Have a blessed week!

Sheila Eismann, Prophetic Seer, Blogger, Author & Teacher, publishes her weekly blog posts endeavoring to encourage others through God's word. Her writings include teaching and instructions on how to apply prophetic insights for daily living. You can subscribe to receive new blog posts on her website at www.sheilaeismann.com.

Sunflowers, Sunshine & Shadows

September 11, 2020
Encouragement

Nature's bounty can provide for many things including a weekly prophetic blog post! Are you encouraged when you see a gorgeous sunflower in bloom? In addition to being the state flower of Kansas and the traditional third wedding anniversary gift, it's beneficial for farmers, birds, and every day living. The seeds are loaded with calcium and other important minerals. If you want to make a good habit of walking in the sunshine instead of the shadows, look to the Son.

https://www.kansasnativeplantsociety.org/stateflower_facts.php

As my husband and I were walking in our neighborhood, we noticed a lone sunflower peeking around the corner to welcome us. It seemed to smile and greet in floral language, "Good morning, and have a nice day!"

When I initially spotted this flower, I was drawn as much to the shadows behind it as I was its gorgeous, inviting bloom. Helen Keller's quote flitted through my spirit, "Keep your face to the sunshine and you cannot see the shadows."

Sunflowers are symbolic of disciples since they follow the sun (God's Son, Jesus Christ). The seeds represent the word of God.

https://sheilaeismann.com/unshakeable/

The positive aspects of shadows are protection and refuge whereas the negative ones can be darkness, sin, and hiding from God.

JoEllen Claypool, fellow author and co-founder of ICAN (Idaho Creative Authors' Network), shares her gardening experience.

"The group of 8 sunflowers took a while to start from seed. I didn't think they were going to make it several times. They looked wilted and not healthy at all. When they were about 2 feet tall, they started perking up a bit. Then they would droop again.

"I started talking to them, 'Come on, girls! You were doing so well. I know you can do this! I know it is unfair that you have to share the nutrients, but whole fields of you do this. I am only asking for 8 of you to share.'

"They started perking up. Then one day, I saw they were all following the sun together, and their tops were all facing the setting sun. I praised them for figuring that out and how beautiful that was. On a few of the very hot days, I saw that they were sad again. I started singing to them, and seriously, the next day their leaves were strong again and not wilted. Such a difference!"

As the summer progressed, I continued to observe our neighborhood sunflower, especially where it was located. It seemed to be planted in a challenging area or perhaps it grew voluntarily, but it was determined to keep growing.

Prophetic Insights for Daily Living:

1. Perhaps we're living in a place we may not have chosen, but we can make a choice to grow, be nourished by Jesus, The Master Gardner, and continue to bloom.

2. Growth takes place when we face the Son and look to His light. (Hebrews 1:3, NIV)

3. We are blessed when we have learned to acclaim the Lord, and walk in the light of His presence. (Psalm 89:15, NIV)

4. Ask yourself if you are viewing the shadows as a positive or a negative. If affirmatively, it's a fabulous idea to pray Psalm 91 aloud every day. The opposite of this could be likened to the past or lurking problems behind us of which no one is exempt. If we keep our eyes on the bright side, we won't be

focusing on the darkness behind us. The past belongs in the past. The only benefit is learning from it and moving on in a positive direction.

5. Just as JoEllen sang to her sunflowers, there are many benefits when we praise the Lord. He loves to hear our voices. The Bible is loaded with verses that pertain to this. Here are a few of them: Psalm 71:8; 103:1; 150:6, and Colossians 3:6.

We can choose to find joy in the simplest, daily pleasures. Our local sunflower was welcoming and projected joy. A companion scripture would be Romans 14:17 which speaks of righteousness, peace, and joy in The Holy Spirit.

As we continue through our week, may we reflect the light of God's love to those who cross our paths because we know He planned for our lives to touch.

There are no coincidences regarding anyone we may meet during our lifetime.

What are some practical steps or actions that you can take to show God's love and be a light in your family, church, or neighborhood?

_____
_____
_____

Keep looking to the Son, fill your hearts with sunshine, and discern the daily shadows. God bless, take care, stay strong, and snack on a few sunflower seeds if you like!

Sheila Eismann, Prophetic Seer, Blogger, Author & Teacher, publishes her weekly blog posts endeavoring to encourage others through God's word. Her writings include teaching and instructions on how to apply prophetic insights for daily living. You can subscribe to receive new blog posts on her website at www.sheilaeismann.com.

The Four Communions

September 16, 2020
Prophetic Teachings

During the time that our state was in the initial stages of Covid-19, we were unable to attend our local church. Thankfully, the services were available online. At the conclusion thereof, my husband and I would take the Lord's Supper. In the following weeks, who would have thought clues would emerge from communion bread?

Having purchased a box of matzo bread at one of our local grocery stores before the outbreak of the "Corona Crud," I broke off a piece each Sunday morning for us to eat along with a small glass of pomegranate juice.

The amazing thing is that I didn't try to force the bread in any particular shape or direction. However, on four different Sundays, the piece I broke for myself ended up closely resembling our state.

Since I'm a native of Idaho, and after the 4th piece pretty much appeared the same as the others, I had to chuckle to myself as I asked God, "Are you trying to tell me something?"

Now, you might be thinking to yourself, "Heaven help you if it took four tries for you to get that simple message!"

The older I'm getting, I'm learning to give myself much more grace. I hope you are, too.

During the Lord's supper, we eat the bread and drink the cup in remembrance of Jesus, our Lord, and Savior. When we participate in this, we should remember what Jesus went through so that our sins could be forgiven, and we could be saved.

"For I received from the Lord that which I also delivered to you: that the Lord Jesus on the *same* night in which He was betrayed took bread; and when He had given thanks, He broke *it* and said, "Take, eat; this is My body which is broken for you; do this in remembrance of Me." In the same manner *He* also *took* the cup after supper, saying, "This cup is the new covenant in My blood. This do, as often as you drink *it,* in remembrance of Me." For as often as you eat this bread and drink this cup, you proclaim the Lord's death till He comes. (1 Corinthians 11:23–26)

While partaking in communion one particular Sunday, I prayed and asked the Lord for the significance of the shape of the bread. The spiritual quickening I received was to increase the intercessory prayer for our state.

Have you sensed the need to pray more often and with greater earnest for your state lately?

_____
_____
_____

Intercession is the act of praying for other people or situations. The Greek noun, *enteuxis* in the Bible is the word for intercession. It primarily denotes a "meeting with," a conversation or petition rendered on behalf of others. "Intercessory prayer," then, is seeking the presence and audience of God in another's stead. When we pray for the needs of others, that is called *intercession* or *intercessory prayer*.

https://biblehub.com/greek/1783.htm

1st Kings 13:6 provides an Old Testament example of an unnamed prophet interceding for Jeroboam, the first king of the northern kingdom, Israel. "Then the king answered and said to the man of God, 'Please entreat the favor of the LORD your God, and pray for me, that my hand may be restored to me.' So the man of God entreated the LORD, and the king's hand was restored to him, and became as before."

In the New Testament, Acts 12:5-11 details the account of the church praying constantly for the Apostle Peter's imprisonment until his dramatic release by an angel of God.

The following list comprises some of the specific ways I've been led to pray for our state during the past few months:

1. Leadership at the local, county, and state levels. When writing to Timothy, a true son in the faith, the Apostle Paul stated in 1st Timothy 2:1-4, "Therefore I exhort first of all that supplications, prayers, intercessions, and giving of thanks be made for all men, for kings and all who are in authority, that we may lead a quiet and peaceable life in all godliness and reverence. For this is good and acceptable in the sight of God our Savior, who desires all men to be saved and to come to the knowledge of the truth." (In this verse, *intercessions* mean approaching [God] with confidence.)

2. Healing for those who've been diagnosed with Covid-19 or any other illness.

3. Health care workers, first responders, and all those on the front lines battling this ongoing pandemic.

4. Comfort for those who've lost loved ones due to any reason.

Wisdom for parents and teachers at all education levels regarding the current school year.

5. Business owners to regain what they've lost.

6. Peace, strength, wisdom, and protection for every person, irrespective of age, who resides within our state boundaries, and that all would come to the saving knowledge of Jesus Christ. (John 3:16)

7. That the land of Idaho would be "married" to the Lord. Isaiah 62:4 reads, "You shall no longer be termed Forsaken, Nor shall your land any more be termed Desolate; But you shall be called Hephzibah, and your land Beulah; For the Lord delights in you, And your land shall be married." [Hephzibah,

meaning "to marry, rule over, possess, or own", and Beulah meaning "my delight is in her" are symbolic names.]

My desire for our state is that it would fulfill its destiny and become all that God intended it to be. Also, every person residing therein would fulfill his or her destiny. It's a sad fact that at the time of the writing of this week's blog post, horrendous wildfires continue to burn in Washington, Oregon, California, and Idaho.

Considering these states, four is symbolic of creation, worldwide, universal, not enough, not bearable, and time (as the fourth dimension.) Pomegranates (we drank the pomegranate juice during communion) represent healing. May God provide what's needed to quench these fires and heal our lands.

Here's another blog post addressing the subject of intercession: https://sheilaeismann.com/the-ox-the-oxbow-the-birdwatcher/

Prophetic Insights for Daily Living:

As you've been interceding for where you live, has God has given you specific prayer directives or strategies? If so, I'd really like to hear from you!

_____
_____
_____

More importantly, as you've prayed, record the results and praises.

The next time you take communion, and if you feel led to do so, please say a special prayer for each of the afore-mentioned states, those battling the fires, and all the residents.

Speaking of participating in the Lord's Supper, look for your clues in communion bread. Have you discovered any?

Prophetic assignments can be fun!

These types of situations and circumstances afford wonderful opportunities to continue with your prophetic journaling to watch how God moves and answers prayers. Thank you, God bless, and take care.

Sheila Eismann, Prophetic Seer, Blogger, Author & Teacher, publishes her weekly blog posts endeavoring to encourage others through God's word. Her writings include teaching and instructions on how to apply prophetic insights for daily living. You can subscribe to receive new blog posts on her website at www.sheilaeismann.com.

The Ox, The Oxbow, & The Birdwatcher

September 23, 2020
Prophetic Teachings

This week's blog post title of "The Ox, The Oxbow & The Birdwatcher" does seem like an odd combination! As I was entreating the Lord at the start of the Jewish New Year 5781 which began on Friday, September 18, 2020, at sundown, this revelatory download began to come forth.

Rosh Hashanah usually appears on calendars as the date marking the Jewish New Year. An important thing to keep in mind is that even if we don't celebrate or pay attention to the Jewish feasts, they still exist on God's calendar. (Leviticus 23:2)

As we close out one year and commence a new one, it's a good time to hit the pause button and reflect upon this past year. There was one extremely ironic aspect to the year of Pey which symbolizes mouth, voice, or open. Pey is the 17th letter of the Hebrew alphabet with a numerical value of 80. Ergo, we are currently in the **decade** of Pey which started September 29th, 2019 in the year 57**80**.

After the pandemic hit America along with other nations, our mouths had to be covered with masks and numerous types of voices were heard across our land, some much louder than others.

Transitioning into this new year, with 9 more "Pey" years ahead of us, the 1st letter (**5781**) of the Hebrew alphabet is Aleph with the symbols of ox, strong, first, to study, and a time to plow.

Oxen have been used since Biblical times. Abraham, Abimelech, and Jacob owned them. (Genesis 12:16; 20:14; and 32:5.) Also, these animals helped to settle the American west and build it, too. They were slower than horses or mules, but they consumed less food, could pull much heavier loads, and required far less maintenance. Sometimes, they had to supply the family's winter meat upon arrival at the chosen destination. In addition, oxen were used to plow fields on the homesteads and in falling trees to build homes.

There are innumerable scripture verses about strength. Balak, king of Moab, said this of God in Numbers 23:22, "He has strength like a wild ox."

King David finalized the theme of Psalm 31, *The Lord, A Fortress in Adversity,* with the verse, "Be of good courage, and He shall strengthen your heart, all you who hope in the Lord."

The two hallmark scriptures which the Lord has given me for the upcoming months are as follows:

2nd Chronicles 16:9a, "For the eyes of the LORD run to and fro throughout the whole earth, to show Himself **strong** on behalf of *those* whose heart is loyal to Him." (Aleph = strong; emphasis mine)

Matthew 18:12-14, "What do you think? If a man has a hundred sheep, and one of them goes astray, does he not leave the ninety-nine and go to the mountains to seek the **one** that is straying? And if he should find it, assuredly, I say to you, he rejoices more over that *sheep* than over the ninety-nine that did not go astray. Even so, it is not the will of your Father who is in heaven that one of these little ones should perish." (Aleph = one; emphasis mine)

I have a wooden recipe holder fashioned in the shape of a rolling pin sitting on my breakfast bar where I place index cards containing important scriptures. These help to serve as reminders and to keep me focused upon the word of the Lord.

The next instruction I received in the Spirit was, "Just like the birdwatcher, become an _oxwatcher_ this year."

Please take note of the places where the emphasis is upon the word ox or contains the word ox.

The Oxbow Dam was quickened unto me. I'm going to be watching for any activity concerning it which is a hydroelectric, rockfill dam on the Snake River bordering Adams County, Idaho, and Baker County, Oregon.

The Bible has a long list of verses regarding strength. For those of you who like to do topical studies, this might be a good suggestion.

This is a year when our strength is going to be challenged, but we must rise to the occasion which will be different for each one of us.

In 2nd Corinthians 12:9, The Apostle Paul reminds us that God's strength is made perfect (mature) in our weakness. When we are weak, we pull on the strength of God. No one person is strong in every area of life. This is why we need God, Jesus, The Holy Spirit, God's word, and each other. In which areas of your life do you need the strength of God to help you?

_____

_____

_____

_____

Perhaps God will bring someone new into your circle of life with strength in the area you need. It will be a divine exchange as you will be able to help provide the strength that person needs. Speaking of circles, it's important to recognize them. Years ago, I wrote a short story about this titled *Recognize Your Circles, A Humorous Look Into Life's Relationships*. Check it out to see if you can relate to any of the characters mentioned!

https://sheilaeismann.com/product/recognize-your-circles-a-humorous-look-into-lifes-relationships/

Prophetic Insights for Daily Living:

Here's a taste of encouragement and instruction for all of us bearing in mind the symbolism for the Hebrew word **Aleph** – (ox, strong, first, to study, and a time to plow) ~~

#1 – In what way(s) will you have to be strong or increase your strength in the year 5781?

_____
_____
_____
_____

#2 – Note the places where God chooses to pour out His strength. Add these to your prophetic journal.

#3 – Keep God, Jesus, and The Holy Spirit first in your life. When we do, everything else will fall into place.

#4 – What is God calling you to study?

_____
_____
_____
_____

#5– Is it a time to plow? If so, you will be given instructions and directives relative to the same. God will provide the equivalent of the oxen.

#6– Who/what are you being assigned or called to watch? This would be of particular interest to Prayer Intercessors.

_____
_____
_____
_____

Happy New Year, and treat yourself to a set of binoculars, a new Bible, writing instrument, or journal!

Sheila Eismann, Prophetic Seer, Blogger, Author & Teacher, publishes her weekly blog posts endeavoring to encourage others through God's word. Her writings include teaching and instructions on how to apply prophetic insights for daily living.

You can subscribe to receive new blog posts on her website at www.sheilaeismann.com.

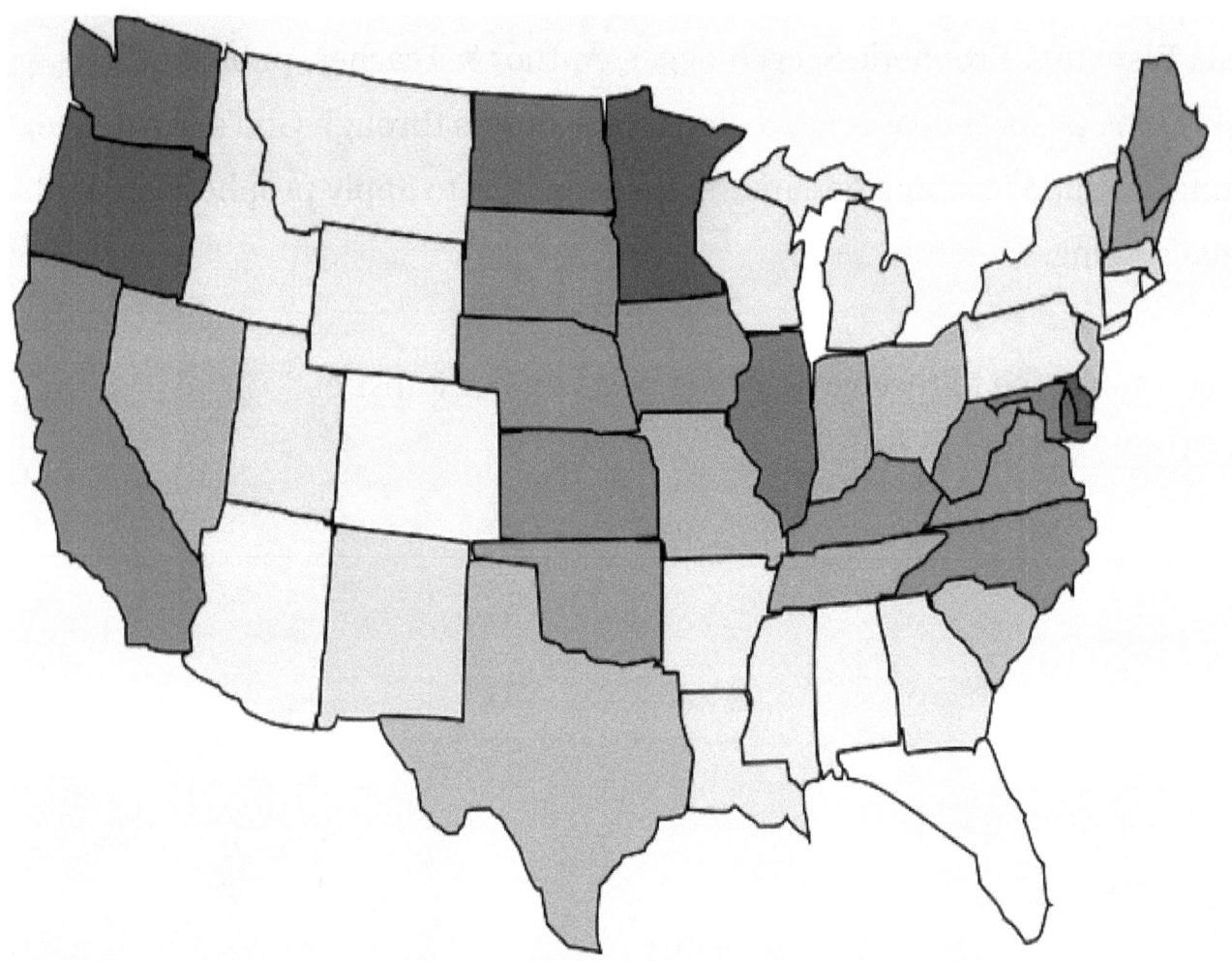

The Forearm, The Torn Map & The Bird's Nest

September 30, 2020
<u>Prophetic Visions</u>

The dark of night had already settled over the mountains on Sunday evening, September 27, 2020, when the prophetic vision unfolded with three spiritual clues: the left forearm, the torn paper map, and the bird's nest.

In the first scene of the vision, the map of the United States was still intact. It resembled one of those similar to what one would see in an elementary school classroom and was taped to a woman's left forearm. The various states appeared in the colors of orange, pink, yellow, red, aqua, beige, blue, sage green, lavender, purple, brown, and forest green.

As I waited on The Holy Spirit, the second scene of the vision emerged wherein the paper map had been torn starting at the very top of the state of Minnesota. The tear extended about halfway down the center of the state.

A few more minutes elapsed; The Spirit opened up, and I saw a tidy nest about 7 inches in diameter which contained three, large, blue-colored, perfectly shaped bird eggs. It reminded me of what someone may discover during the springtime of the year.

Then the vision ended. Since the hour was getting late, I made notations of what I'd seen in The Spirit.

Regarding the map, a further revelation was not given to me as to how or by whom it had been torn, but it was a fresh or recent tear. Upon closer examination of this, it would appear that it started in Koochiching County and progressed down through the following additional counties: Itasca, Cass, Aitkin, Crow Wing, Morrison, Mille Lacs, and Kanabec within the state of Minnesota.

Never having physically lived in that geographic region of our country, I'm unsure as to the significance or history and background of that particular area.

In some sense, it's rather strange that the map was taped to a person's forearm as opposed to just hanging on a wall or suspended in mid-air.

Before we take a look-see at the symbolism of this vision, I wanted to mention something vital concerning the spiritual gifts of which there are three basic categories:

The 9 Holy Spirit gifts outlined in 1 Corinthians 12:4-11;

The 5-Fold Ministry gifts which Jesus bestowed upon the church as listed in Ephesians 4:11-12; and

The Ministry or Motivational Gifts are listed in Romans 12:3-8.

The Apostle Paul reminds us in Romans 12:6 which states that "if prophecy, let us *prophesy* in proportion to our faith,"

In other words, concerning any aspect of the prophetic realm, we stop when the revelation we receive from The Holy Spirit stops. We add no flesh to it because the flesh profits nothing. (John 6:63)

We balance this with Proverbs 25:2, "It is the glory of God to conceal a matter, but the glory of kings is to search out a matter." As Christians, we are kings and priests under the New Covenant according to Revelation 1:5e-6, "To Him [Jesus] who loved us and washed us from our sins in His own blood, and has made us kings and priests to His God and Father, to Him be glory and dominion forever and ever. Amen."

It's incumbent to search out and pray into the prophetic things with which we are entrusted. One of the ways to search out a matter is to plug in the prophetic symbolism to the extent that we can. As we pray into the dreams and visions, we can ask God for the interpretation thereof. (Genesis 40:8)

Maps are symbolic of:

Seeking directions
Guidance
Plan for your life
Wanting to know where we are in the plan of God.

Since this was a map of America, I deem the applicable symbol is the last one listed. Where are we in the plan of God? What's the prophetic timetable for the United States?

A most unfortunate incident occurred in Minneapolis earlier this year which has led to even more unrest and tearing of our nation.

https://sheilaeismann.com/spirit-of-lawlessness/

Back to the vision of the torn map for a moment, it's most intriguing that the tear started at the top of the state.

Arms typify strength or influence. Left signifies intellect, soul, teaching, foolishness, carefree, casual, riches and honor (left side of wisdom), heart, weakness, and flesh. The arm or forearm and strength are usually associated with a man rather than a woman; however, the map was taped to the forearm of a woman. She was bearing the map, so to speak.

The bird's nest with the three eggs is quite intriguing to follow the map sequence. The nest represents a place of security, especially for the young, and eggs symbolize promises, new beginnings, gifts, schemes, and plans. We definitely welcome the most positive aspect of the number three: the trinity (God the Father, Jesus the Son, and The Holy Spirit); complete; and resurrection.

In the vision, the eggs had not yet hatched. What could that telegraph or represent? Also, since they were blue, which is the color of heaven, what clues can we glean?

_____

_____

_____

_____

We should keep a sharp eye on this prophetic vision as we wind down this year and head into the spring of next year as to who or what emerges from the state of Minnesota. It could also be that three things are "hatched" or "birthed" next spring.

In addition, I deem it's important to keep a bird's eye view of the state of South Dakota.

Things that are torn need to be mended. We can draw encouragement from Ecclesiastes 3:7a, "a time to tear and a time to mend;" (NIV) The historical aspect to this verse comes from 2nd Samuel 13:31. When bad news was received, it was customary to rip one's garment to show grief and mourning. When the problem or situation passed, it was prudent to sew the garment back together.

God, in His omnipotence, can mend anything that has been torn. He responds to the prayers and pleas of His people.

Granted, most maps are made of paper. When searching the symbolism for this, the one which leaped off the page was **_plans._**

Based upon the vision, it would appear as though the tearing was intentional by someone. But, even if it was, God can rectify this if we entreat Him with humble hearts and spirits. Spring of 2021 may seem like a long way off, but time goes by in the blink of an eye!

Prophetic Insights for Daily Living:

1. Please join me in praying for our nation. If you're inclined and/or able to do so, travel to your state's capital. As you stand on the grounds, thank God for your state, the spiritual clues He gives us, and offer prayers and petitions as you are led by The Holy Spirit. Then, watch and record what follows!

_____
_____
_____
_____

2. Print off a colored map of our country. As you trace your fingers across each state, ask God to bless each one, the residents therein, and for His peace to settle across our land.

3. Record specifically what God shows you concerning the tearing of the map. Also, why it was taped to the forearm of a woman.

_____

_____

_____

_____

4. Purpose in your heart to be a part of the mending solution as opposed to the tearing problem. When I worked in a law firm decades ago, there was a quotation printed in large, bold font and taped to one of the walls in the office which read, "If you're not part of the solution, you're part of the problem." I'm not finding nearly as much humor in it now as I did when I first read it.

Be encouraged in the Lord and in the power of His might. Have a blessed week.

Sheila Eismann, Prophetic Seer, Blogger, Author & Teacher, publishes her weekly blog posts endeavoring to encourage others through God's word. Her writings include teaching and instructions on how to apply prophetic insights for daily living. You can subscribe to receive new blog posts on her website at www.sheilaeismann.com.

Cindy, Dean & The Test

October 7, 2020
Prophetic Dreams

There are times when I receive a dream, and some clues for the interpretation can reside within the meaning of a person's name. Such is the case for this week's blog post titled "Cindy, Dean & The Test."

In scene one of my dream on Sunday morning, October 4, 2020, I was sleeping in my bedroom although it was not my bedroom in real life. This room was expansive and was paneled all around with dark, cherry wood. The furniture was the same color.

While still in the dream, I awakened to find Cindy sitting at the head of the bed. In real life, I'd met her several years ago, and her general appearance was the same as when I first saw her.

I was aghast when I discovered that she'd taken the liberty to go through my brown briefcase which contained all of my personal information. I don't know how she got inside the room. She was looking for Dean Kunz and was confident that I knew him and his whereabouts. The Spirit zoomed in several times on his name such as when you would use binoculars to look at something in greater detail.

Disclaimer – if Dean Kunz is your name in real life, this dream does not apply to you. Again, I deem the name was given to me to assist with interpretation using the meaning of the names. I don't know anyone named Dean Kunz. In fact, I'd never heard the name before I received the dream.

In the second scene, I needed to take a test that was being proctored by specific individuals. I entered the facility looking for a place to sit down and spread my materials out before the test began. The room was very cramped inside, and I could not easily find a spot.

A second challenge surfaced as I needed to use the restroom before the start time. It was more difficult to find a bathroom stall than a seat in a chair or at a table to take the test.

Finally, I found a restroom stall. Even though I was in a very deep sleep, I could feel myself emptying my bladder which lasted for several minutes.

In the last scene of the dream, my garments supernaturally changed to where I was adjusting a new, cotton, knit summer top which had a patriotic theme of red, white, and blue. The top had an overlapping collar which was approximately 7 inches wide with blue and red stars appliqued on a white background. The left side of the collar was tucked underneath the fabric, so I had to reach in, pull it out, and lay it flat across my collar bone. My mother, who's now in heaven, had gifted me this top.

The dream ended just as I was getting settled to finally take the test.

Symbolism pertaining to this dream:

#1. It was given to me on the 4th day of the month. Four is symbolic of worldwide, creation, universal, rule or dominion, time (the fourth dimension), the spirit realm (the fourth dimension), or open door (Revelation 4:1 – a door standing open in heaven.)

#2. Bedroom – location of the dream. Symbols are privacy, intimacy, inner circle and to confide in, and the place of heart communion.

#3. Cindy:

Literal meaning: Goddess of the Moon

Suggested Character Quality: Reflector of Light

Suggested Lifetime Scripture Verse: Psalm 27:1, "The Lord is my light and salvation; whom shall I fear? The Lord is the stronghold of my life; of whom shall I be afraid?" (Explanation: The moon reflects the light of the sun; we are to reflect God's Son, Jesus Christ.)

A person's characteristics can be another important clue whether it's someone we know in real life or just somebody who appears in a dream. Cindy is the type of person who's very intrusive into people's lives. At first blush, one would not suspect this as she seemed to spend most of her time decorating her lovely, expensive home. Also, she desired to be a socialite, but there was another side to her wherein she would drill deep into a situation or circumstance to find out what was going on.

#4. Dean:

Literal meaning: Dweller in the valley

Suggested Character Quality: Courageous Spirit

Suggested Lifetime Scripture Verse: Psalm 16:8, "I have placed the Lord before me continually; because He is at my right hand, I shall not be moved."

#5. Kunz – the meaning is an honest advisor.

#6. Test – it was not revealed to me in the dream as to the exact type of test I was required to take; however, it was a test, nonetheless.

#7. Bathroom – cleansing, conviction, repentance, or refreshing. The bladder is part of the excretory system. In Jeremiah 31:20, the Hebrew word is *me 'ah* and used figuratively for the place of emotions or distress or love.

#8. Patriotic clothing – it was a gift from my mother who can be symbolized by the church, The Holy Spirit, a spiritual mother, nurturer, or a natural mother. Clothing in a dream can also represent our attitude, depict the state of our relationship with God, or indicate the state of one's heart.

Prophetic Insights for Daily Living:

Most of the applications of this dream apply to a test.

#1. Plugging in Cindy's name – If you are fearful, of whom are you afraid? The only fear we are to have is the holy, reverential fear of God.

Fear of man is a trap and a snare. (Proverbs 29:25) "The name of the LORD is a strong tower; the righteous run to it and are safe." (Proverbs 18:10; Psalm 62:2)

https://sheilaeismann.com/dream-therapy/

Cindy was looking through my personal belongings.

She was confident that I knew Dean Kunz and his whereabouts.

#2. Concerning Dean Kunz – courageous spirit and bold advisor.

a. Do we have a courageous spirit, and who is our advisor? The best advisors we can have are God, Jesus Christ, The Holy Spirit, and the word of God.

b. If we don't already have a courageous spirit, we're definitely going to need one for the days ahead.

c. Have we placed the Lord continually before us as He needs to be our focus? If so, we will not be moved amid the tumult and chaos.

d. The name Dean Kunz is sort of a double play on words of courageous spirit and bold advisor. Granted, we can have a natural person who's a courageous and bold advisor. But the REAL courage and boldness come from having Jesus within us. The righteous are as bold as a lion (Proverbs 28:1) and retreat before nothing (Proverbs 30:30 – NIV). Since Jesus is the Lion of the Tribe of Judah (Revelation 5:5), may He arise within us!

#3. Our emotions – are we storing them within us in an unhealthy manner or are we ridding ourselves of them? When we use the bathroom, we "void" our bodies of the toxins, excess, build-ups, etc. (Part of me hesitated to mention this portion of the dream, but since it was such an integral part of it, I decided to include it.

Also, it's rare when having a dream and being in a deep state of REM that people can actually experience the equivalent of the same thing as when they are wide awake.)

#4. Challenge – It was a challenge to find a bathroom stall and a place to sit before taking the test. Are we up to these challenges or are you facing any?

#5. Patriotic clothing – our first allegiance is to King Jesus and His kingdom on earth.

In the dream, the left side of the collar of the new patriotic knit top had to be adjusted and turned right side out. Will we pass the test and remain patriotic?

The collar is placed around our neck which is symbolic of will. The surrendering of our will to God's will is a supreme challenge in itself.

America is a gift from God. Do we view it in that manner?

Many prayers are being offered on behalf of our nation right now. I'm reminded of Psalm 66:18 which exhorts us, "If I regard iniquity in my heart, the Lord will not hear."

With courageous spirits, let's lift our eyes, hearts, and voices toward heaven and pass the test, shall we?

Let's stand up for America!

Also, I invite you to pray about the interpretation of this dream. How does it speak to you or what is your takeaway from it?

_____
_____
_____
_____

For those of you who have just started prophetic journaling, a suggestion would be to print this blog post which touches on the subject of prophetic dream interpretation.

As you embark upon a new day, God desires to bless you. He wants you to have joy, peace, hope, and most of all, the absolute reassurance of His love and comfort through His Son and The Holy Spirit.

Sheila Eismann, Prophetic Seer, Blogger, Author & Teacher, publishes her weekly blog posts endeavoring to encourage others through God's word. Her writings include teaching and instructions on how to apply prophetic insights for daily living. You can subscribe to receive new blog posts on her website at www.sheilaeismann.com.

Two Ladies, Reptiles & Horses

October 14, 2020
Prophetic Visions

Studying prophetic symbols can be challenging and rewarding. This week's blog post sets the stage for such an exercise.

A set of scales appeared before me in The Spirit on Friday afternoon, October 9, 2020. If one were to look straight at them, the left tray was 6 inches higher than the right one. The scales were supernaturally suspended in mid-air.

Attached to the left tray was a slender snake approximately a foot in length that was covered with gold. Its small, top, gold-colored teeth were clenched as it gripped the rim of the tray.

The vision proceeded slowly down the snake until it got to the tip of its tail wherein its feet resembled those of a lizard. The 5 small toes were pressing hard on the right side of the tray of the set of scales to keep them down.

Suddenly, a rider on a solid bay-colored horse, a white snip on its nose, and a white stocking on its right rear leg approached the set of scales. He drew his sword from his sheath and severed the snake in half which caused its insides to fly into the air. The internal substance was composed of a metal, mesh, tightly woven, cable-looking substance. What it reminded me of was a drain cable my husband once purchased when repairing our dishwasher. Normal snakes have many small bones or vertebrae throughout their body, but this was no normal snake!

When the lead rider, or captain, severed the snake, a victorious shout could be heard from similar riders who'd just arrived on horseback. Each horse was identical. Having been the office manager for a National Horse Breed Registry a few decades ago, finding horses with identical markings would be really rare.

The riders wore unusual helmets. There was a metal band across the top closely resembling the crown on the Statue of Liberty located on Liberty Island in Upper New York Bay off the coast of New York City.

Engraved on the crown were the words **LIBERTY WARRIORS**.
Then the vision ended.

This is quite the set of eclectic symbols to plug in when praying about an interpretation!

Sometimes, a prophetic dream or vision is given which pertains to something that's happening in real-time in the earth or God's kingdom.

I'm listing the objects or people in the order in which they appeared in the vision and the symbolism related to each one:

#1. Scales – Suffice it to say, scales are used for many different purposes. If this pertains to the scales of justice, *Lady Justice* is to be blind. She holds the scales in her right hand and a sword in her left. The sword is always lower than the scales because punishment should only happen after the evidence is accurately weighed. The blindfold she wears should represent our justice system which is supposed to be blind to someone's gender, race, power, and wealth.

Perhaps you've heard the saying, "Someone had their thumb on the scales . . ." In this vision, the lizard had its toes on the scales.

Toes – power and dominion; drive and influence; leverage; leadership.

#2. The Number 6 – Image; man; flesh; carnal; idol; form; human; humanity in independence and opposition to God (flesh or sin); not of God; works.

#3. Snake – Curse; demon; evil spirit; deception; threat; danger; hatred; slander; critical spirit; witchcraft.

A skinny snake is a curse of poverty.

The most unusual aspect of this snake that appeared in the vision was the lizard toes. Most snakes do not have toes. On September 17, 2009, *Popular Science* reported an article about a snake with a clawed foot; however, it was uncertain as to whether or not it was a mutation or a fabrication. Also, with the snake featured in the article, it showed a weird clawed limb sticking out of its side as opposed to being at the tail end of the snake.

Some boas and pythons have one single toe attached to the pelvic area, but not at the tip of the tail.

On a side note, I've wondered if the serpent which appeared in the Garden of Eden to tempt Eve had at one time walked upright.

Genesis 3:14 reads,

"So the Lord God said to the serpent:

"Because you have done this,
You *are* cursed more than all cattle,
And more than every beast of the field;
On your belly you shall go,
And you shall eat dust
All the days of your life."

If the snake had always slithered on the ground, why would the curse contain the specific language of, "On your belly you shall go?"

If it had walked upright originally, it most probably would have had toes.

#4. Gold – Glory or wisdom; truth; something precious; righteousness; glory of God; self-glorification. The snake (evil spirit) was covered with gold. Even though its outward appearance was gold, evil lurked beneath the covering.

#5. Teeth – Animal's Teeth – danger; predator. The snake's real teeth were covered with gold. The same application listed in **#4** would apply here.

#6. – Lizard – Unclean spirit. There are many verses in the Bible about this subject.
Some of them are:

Zechariah 13:2
Matthew 12:43
Mark 1:23, 26; 3:30; 5:2; 5:8 and 7:25.
Luke 4:33; 9:42; and 11:24.
Revelation 18:2

#7. – Horse – Time/work; flesh; spiritual warfare; strength; power; and authority.

#8. – Sword – Words; Word of God; critical words; evil intent; threat; strife; war; persecution; divides and separates.

I've watched a few episodes of the tv series *Forged in Fire*, and I've not witnessed a knife that could cut through gold; however, there may be one that exists.

#9. – Cable – A cable transmits something. In this case, the transmission was from a snake to a lizard, both of which symbolize evil or unclean spirits. The demonic spirits are working in tandem and communicating through the cable to keep the left side of the scale elevated.

#10. – Helmet – Salvation; hope; protect your mind; spiritual warfare.

#11. – Statue of Liberty – The original name was *Liberty Enlightening the World.* Lady Liberty represents freedom. True freedom is found in following Jesus, God's only begotten Son, Who declared in John 8:32, "And you shall know the truth, and the truth shall make you free."

Symbolism of the Statue of Liberty – Freedom and spiritual deliverance.

#12. – Crown – Authority or reward; rule; honor; glory; power; promotion. Kings wear crowns, and Christians are referred to as kings and priests in Revelation 1:6 and 5:10. Believers are promised various crowns in scripture. They serve as the reminder of the eternal rewards for those who faithfully serve God while on earth.

#13. – Two Ladies – It's interesting that this vision sort of pertains to two ladies: Lady Justice and Lady Liberty. Justice is needed to have true liberty. Also, liberty is needed to have true justice.

Since I was raised with an agricultural background, I'll plug in an appropriate adage here, "Water runs both ways through the pipe on this one!"

When addressing the church at Thessalonica, the Apostle Paul exhorted them in 1 Thessalonians 5:19-22, "Do not quench the Spirit. Do not despise prophecies. Test all things; hold fast what is good. Abstain from every form of evil."

Prophetic Insights for Daily Living:

As you've read through this blog post, what comes to mind for you?

_____
_____
_____
_____

Do you deem it has a present-day application? If so, what would that be?

_____
_____
_____
_____

In the prophetic realm of dreams and visions, objects and people can manifest in many different forms. What's relevant and important about the symbols in this prophetic vision?

_____
_____
_____
_____

Why do you think the snake is keeping its foot on the lower tray of the scale? Who or what is it trying to influence?

_____
_____
_____
_____

How do you feel led to pray?

_____
_____
_____
_____

What portion of the Word of God would be best and most applicable to study?

_____
_____
_____
_____

If it's not your usual practice to look into studying prophetic symbols, this week's blog post serves up a good one for doing just that.

Spiritual food for thought: The evil spirit was able to continue to manipulate the scales until the Liberty Warrior rode up and severed it in half.

It's time to go on the offense. RIDERS UP!

https://sheilaeismann.com/snare-alert/

Sheila Eismann, Prophetic Seer, Blogger, Author & Teacher, publishes her weekly blog posts endeavoring to encourage others through God's word. Her writings include teaching and instructions on how to apply prophetic insights for daily living. You can subscribe to receive new blog posts on her website at www.sheilaeismann.com.

A Reed Shaken In The Wind

October 21, 2020
Prophetic Visions

How would you describe 2020 thus far? Have you felt like it's been one of those Hebrews 12:27-29 seasons wherein only that which cannot be shaken can and will remain? Have you felt like a reed shaken in the wind or are you remaining unshakeable?

Within the past couple of days, I've been drawn into the Spirit wherein I saw the vertebral column or backbone of a human.

In the next scene of the vision, a steel rod was supernaturally affixed to this column.

Then I heard, "This is what it's going to take to stand in the days ahead."

As I pondered this vision, several scriptures were quickened unto me. The first one was the Biblical account found in Luke 7:19-24 wherein John the Baptist sent two of his disciples to Jesus asking Him, "Are you the Coming One, or do we look for another?" After curing many in attendance of infirmities, afflictions, evil spirits, lameness, and blindness, Jesus told the disciples to report back to John what they'd seen and heard.

After John's disciples departed, Jesus addressed the multitudes which remained. He asked, "What did you go into the wilderness to see? A reed shaken in the wind?"

Why do reeds blow in the wind? Implementing the first part of the vision I received, it's because they have no backbone. They are subject to the wind and do whatever it wants. This analogy could be applied to those who subject themselves to whatever wind is presently blowing irrespective of the arena, whether it be political, educational, financial, environmental, etc. In addition, when the winds of adversity begin to blow, they change direction with it.

One could opine that John the Baptist most assuredly had a backbone of steel. He spoke strongly of repentance from sin and was ultimately beheaded because of his stance. (Matthew 14:1-12) Suffice it to say, he was the furthest thing from a reed shaken in the wind.

Jesus was addressing the multitude with rhetorical questions regarding John the Baptist. He asked them what they had gone into the wilderness to see. I would dare say most everyone in the region already knew John's reputation.

Even with King Herod breathing death threats against John the Baptist, he did not quake in his boots or bend like a reed in the wind. He stood firm and unmovable in his convictions and beliefs.

If we are as weak as a reed, we will shake like a reed. If we are strong in our spirits, we will remain so with the help of Jesus Christ our Lord, and The Holy Spirit Who indwells believers. (1st Corinthians 3:16 and 6:19)
When we are resolute in mind and spirit, we can still have peace amid chaos and a raging storm. The way this is achieved is spelled out for us:

Isaiah 26:3-4, "You will keep *him* in perfect peace,
Whose mind *is* stayed *on You,*
Because he trusts in You.
Trust in the Lord forever,
For in Yah, the Lord, *is* everlasting strength."

Peace is also one of the fruits of the Spirit in our lives. (Galatians 5:22) I can usually tell which one of the nine fruits The Holy Spirit is working on within me because there will be a lack thereof or a challenge that surfaces. Thankfully, He does not require me to be working on all of them at once!

Jesus is our peace. (Ephesians 2:14) Do we look to Him in the midst of our storms? He's always in the boat with us whether we see Him there or not. (Mark 4:35-41)

When writing to the church at Philippi, the Apostle Paul exhorted them, "Be anxious for nothing, but in everything by prayer and supplication, with thanksgiving, let your requests be made known to God; and the peace of God, which surpasses all understanding, will guard your hearts and minds through Christ Jesus." (Philippians 4:6-7)

I would like to ask you this question, "When is the last time you were anxious for nothing?"

It's been pretty tough for all of us to remain free from worry and anxiety during a worldwide pandemic.

From a psychological standpoint and since most battles occur in the theatre of the mind, I would like to suggest that it's important to have something to look forward to each day even if it seems minute or insignificant. Peace, contentment, and faith are controlled by our minds and thought processes. They will help to ensure that we don't become a shaken reed.

https://sheilaeismann.com/three-cs-the-closet-canoe-calm/

Prophetic Insights for Daily Living:

Fix a cup of tea and meditate upon scriptures about peace.
Call a friend for mutual encouragement or prayer support.

Observe birds, squirrels, falling leaves, or some sort of nature that offers its own kind of peace.

Color a page from your adult coloring book. I especially enjoy Lila's Garden https://www.amazon.com/Lilas-Garden-Cottage-Coloring-Book/dp/1530810426/ref=sr_1_3?dchild=1&keywords=Lila%27s+Garden+by+Cathie+Richardson&qid=1603297288&sr=8-3

Write a note or send a card to someone to share your love.

Read an inspirational book.

Listen to and sing along with praise music.

Do something kind for someone who least expects it.

Spend some time on a hobby or project.

Go for a walk, run, or bike ride. Physical exercise greatly reduces stress.

Prayer is the most important one on this list along with reading the word of God. He created us to stay in communication with Him. The best part is that He's available 24/7. He never takes a vacation!

What other things would you add to the aforementioned list?

_____

_____

_____

_____

Peace is a precious possession. We can't allow the things going on in our world to destroy it.

My prayer for all of us is that we will not be as a reed shaken in the wind, will have backbones of steel when needed, and remain calm and peaceful.

Since God is unshakeable, when we put our trust in Him **alone**, we will not be shaken by the systems of this world.

"Therefore take up the whole armor of God, that you may be able to withstand in the evil day, and having done all, to stand." (Ephesians 6:13)

Are you standing or shaking? If you're shaking, what's causing you to do so?
_____
_____
_____
_____

If you're standing, Who or what is helping you to stand?
_____
_____
_____
_____

How have you felt directed by The Holy Spirit to help you stand in Jesus Christ our Lord and have a backbone of steel?
_____
_____
_____
_____

Sheila Eismann, Prophetic Seer, Blogger, Author & Teacher, publishes her weekly blog posts endeavoring to encourage others through God's word. Her writings include teaching and instructions on how to apply prophetic insights for daily living. You can subscribe to receive new blog posts on her website at www.sheilaeismann.com.

Trapped by the Trappings
October 28, 2020
Prophetic Warnings

Prepositions are such small words, but every once in a while, they can make a huge difference! On Friday evening, October 23rd, 2020, around 8:20 ish p.m., I heard from The Holy Spirit, "Trapped **by** the trappings." I sensed that He wanted me to pay particular attention to the exact wording, especially the two-letter preposition within the wording. At first blush, and when one thinks of something being trapped, it's usually in a trap, not by a trap. Hence, this snare alert!

As I waited for further direction, I suddenly realized the instructions I received pertained more to the spiritual aspect of things rather than the physical, although there's usually a parallel between them.

The enemy of our souls has many hooks, snares, lures, and traps with which to catch us. Three of the main ones are:

#1. The lust of the flesh.

#2. The lust of the eyes.

#3. The pride of life.

"For all that *is* in the world—the lust of the flesh, the lust of the eyes, and the pride of life—is not of the Father but is of the world." (1 John 2:16) Pride has its own set of problems, but that's a different message for another time.

Once we're caught in the trap of the lust of the flesh and the lust of the eyes, i.e., covetousness, our souls and spirits begin to diminish. We lose our strength as we fight to break free. If we are unable to do so, it can cling to us like spiritual leprosy.

What are trappings anyway? Here's the definition: articles of equipment or dress, especially of an ornamental character; conventional adornment; characteristic signs. An important synonym is raiment.

https://www.dictionary.com

Stated another way: the outward signs, features, or objects associated with a particular situation, role, or thing.

The 5th chapter of 2 Kings is most instructive when addressing this subject. The major characters within are Naaman, commander of the army of the king of Syria; a Jewish servant girl; the prophet Elisha; and his servant, Gehazi. As we read completely through this portion of scripture, it's fascinating that God embeds some intentional situations, choices, tests, and outcomes.

Unfortunately, when the narrative opens, Naaman had leprosy. It's a chronic, progressive, bacterial infection that affects primarily the nerves of the skin, lining of the nose, upper respiratory tract, and extremities. It's also known as Hansen's disease which can produce skin ulcers, muscle weakness, and nerve damage. If left untreated, it can cause extreme disability and severe disfigurement. WHO developed a multi-drug therapy in 1995 to help cure leprosy of which there are three basic types; however, this was of little value in the year 860 B.C.

Through the initial suggestion of the Jewish servant girl, the king of Syria eventually sent a letter to the king of Israel requesting that he heal Naaman. Thankfully, Elisha intervened with the directive and word of the Lord for Naaman's healing.

When the instructions were delivered, Naaman flew into a rage, but his servant finally talked some sense into him. After Naaman obeyed God's commands, he was completely healed which was a miracle! The most important aspect is that Naaman's heart, in part, turned to the God of Israel.

Naaman offered Elisha a gift who promptly refused it. A true prophet of God discerns when to take a gift and when to decline it.

After Naaman departed, Gehazi, Elisha's servant, acted upon his growing greed and ran after Naaman. Spinning a long yarn about two young men from the mountains of Ephraim needing some supplies, he convinced Naaman to fork over two talents of silver and two changes of garments which Naaman's servants carried all the way to the citadel for Gehazi. He quickly hid them in the house. Gehazi lied the first time to Naaman, and a second time to his master, Elisha, when asked about his recent travels.

Elisha, calling Gehazi to account, knew full well what he'd done. After asking him a rhetorical question, the prophet pronounced God's judgment upon Gehazi as he was instantly struck with leprosy from which Naaman had been miraculously healed.

As I dug deeper into this passage of scripture, I was reminded of the wisdom and balance that life requires. Here are some things for us to keep in mind:

Since the earth is the Lord's and the fullness thereof (Psalm 24:1), there's nothing wrong with receiving the blessings of the Lord.

According to Deuteronomy 8:18, "And you shall remember the Lord your God, for *it is* He who gives you power to get wealth, that He may establish His covenant which He swore to your fathers, as *it is* this day."

A. 1st Timothy 6:10 – it's the **love of money** that's the root of all kinds of evil. Money, in and of itself, is not evil. Consider how God richly blessed Abraham. (Genesis 13.2)

B. Extreme wealth is actually a test from God to see what we will do with it and how we will steward the same.

C. Jesus warned us that we cannot serve both Him and money. (Matthew 6:24) There's something specifically tied to money that's a powerful trap to our souls and spirits. This is why Jesus spoke as He did. We are forced to choose Whom or what we will serve.

D. Since God is our Jehovah-Jireh (Genesis 22:14), He will supply all of our needs (not greeds) according to His riches in glory by Christ Jesus. (Philippians 4:19)

E. When addressing a crowd, Jesus warned them in Luke 12:15, "And He said to them, "Take heed and beware of **covetousness,** for one's life does not consist in the abundance of the things he possesses." (Emphasis mine)

F. "So the eyes of man are never satisfied." (Proverbs 27:20b)

G. According to the Apostle Paul, godliness with contentment is great gain. (1 Timothy 6:6)

While it can be a supreme challenge to wait upon the Lord for Him to provide and move at His discretion for increase, business opportunities, etc., we'll be a whole lot better off in the long run if we do, so we can use our wealth wisely within His kingdom.

https://sheilaeismann.com/dream-therapy/

Another uncanny aspect to this whole story emerged when I consulted the meanings of the names Naaman and Gehazi.

Naaman's name means pleasant, pleasantness, or satisfaction. (Genesis 46:21)

1. Due to his position as commander of Syria's army, Naaman exhibited pride through his attitude and actions.

2. Initially he was snared through #3 above (the pride of life), but when he humbled himself and obeyed God through the word of His prophet, he prospered.

3. He passed the spiritual test, in part. (2 Kings 5:15-19)

4. Imagine how pleasant it was when Naaman's unpleasant leprosy suddenly vanished!

The name Gehazi means valley of sight or vision. (2 Kings 4:12)

1. He was ensnared by #2 above – the lust of the eyes.

2. The silver trapped him. This ties back to the love of money.

3. One talent was an enormous amount of silver which was equal to 3,000 shekels or about 70 pounds. As of May 2020, the approximate price of silver was $206.51 per pound. Ergo, we're talking around $14,456 in today's economy.

4. Naaman offered two sets of raiments (articles of dress) which Gehazi greedily accepted along with the silver whereas the prophet Elisha flatly refused ten talents of silver, six thousand shekels of gold, and ten changes of clothing. (2 Kings 5:5)

5. When he allowed greed to overtake him, Gehazi lost sight of what's important and true spiritual vision. He was running after Naaman (pleasantness or satisfaction), but it was in the wrong direction with the incorrect motive.

6. Gehazi was discontent. He didn't appreciate his current assignment from God which was to serve his master, Elisha, who issued a stern rebuke in verse 26 of the chapter, "*Is it* time to receive money and to receive clothing **(trappings, raiment, dress)**, olive groves and vineyards, sheep and oxen,

male and female servants?" Suffice it to say, if God would have wanted Gehazi to have those things, He would have most certainly provided them. Gehazi flunked the test. (Emphasis and insertion mine)

7. 2 Kings 5:27 reads, "The leprosy of Naaman shall cling to you and your descendants forever." Plugging in the meaning of Naaman's name, pleasantness and satisfaction left Gehazi when leprosy arrived. Unpleasantness and dissatisfaction were to be his constant condition for the remainder of his days on earth.

8. The verdict pronounced upon Gehazi was for him and his descendants forever. Our spiritual decisions affect our future generations and legacies.

Prophetic Insights for Daily Living:

1 Corinthians 10:11 and Romans 15:4 remind us that scripture is written for our instruction and admonition from which we draw wisdom, strength, and whatever else we need at the time.

King Solomon, the wisest man who ever lived, said it best in Proverbs 4:23, "Above all else, guard your heart, for it is the wellspring of life."

If covetousness can lead to (spiritual) leprosy, that's not something I want or need. Lord, please help us to keep a sharp eye on the lures, snares, and traps. We are confident that You will provide for us in Your way and in Your time. May we make wise choices unlike Gehazi whose eyes locked onto the silver and garment trappings, and his life was never the same after that.

God's resounding displeasure concerning covetousness is crystal clear. Naaman received healing from leprosy, and Gehazi did not.

In evaluating this prophetic warning, how could you or someone else possibly be trapped by the trappings?

_____
_____
_____
_____

Some gold is fool's gold, and silver can be seductive.

Who's offering what to you, if anything, or what are you pursuing?

_____
_____
_____
_____

If you watch the national news, can you think of anyone who's been trapped by the trappings? If so, who was this, and what was the account thereof? What is the lesson(s) to be learned? Have you prayed for those involved?

_____
_____
_____
_____

Sheila Eismann, Prophetic Seer, Blogger, Author & Teacher, publishes her weekly blog posts endeavoring to encourage others through God's word. Her writings include teaching and instructions on how to apply prophetic insights for daily living. You can subscribe to receive new blog posts on her website at www.sheilaeismann.com.

The Closet, Canoe & Calm
November 2, 2020
Prophetic Visions

Prophetic visions can sometimes contain an odd assortment of symbols, so this one would be no exception! Let's see if we can connect the dots of the three C's: the closet, canoe, and calm, shall we? I was intrigued as I dug deeper.

Scene #1: A coiled rattle snake appeared in a master bedroom closet. The door was open, so you could fully see the serpent. It had very seductive eyes with extraordinarily long eye lashes which batted up and down. Its mouth was closed, but the rattles could be heard. It was ready to strike! It's interesting to note that since its mouth was closed, it did not speak as in Genesis Chapter 3. The emphasis was more upon its eyes rather than its mouth or voice.

Symbolism for 1st Scene:

A. Snake – sin; a person who speaks poisonous words; satan; evil spirit; curse; a tempter; lying spirit; deception; false teacher.

B. Eyes – a window to the soul which reveals what's in the heart; desire (good or evil); covetousness; passion; lust; revelation and understanding.

C. Bedroom – private; intimacy or union; inner circle as someone in whom you would confide; the place of communion; covenant – good or bad; natural or spiritual adultery.

D. Closet – private; secret; place of prayer; hidden sins from the past; heart; storage; thoughts (the mind); delay; reserve or preserve; abundance; hidden; accumulated.

Scene #2: In the next scene of the vision, I saw a husband and wife inside a canoe. They had chosen it from a large selection stored on a secluded, sandy beach. Burned into the wood on the front of the canoe was Romans 12:18.

Symbolism for 2nd Scene:

A. Canoe – Undeveloped (primitive) ministry or person; the flesh; ministry in our own strength; life's journey; Holy Spirit transport; Holy Spirit led individual (moving without the paddle in running water).
B. Romans 12:18 – "If it is possible, as much as depends on you, live peaceably with all men."
C. Husband and wife – head of a family; marriage; covenant.

Scene #3: The last scene opened to where the canoe was gently floating in scenic, serene waters. I did not see any paddles for the canoe.

Symbolism for 3rd Scene:

A. Water – Spirit of God; word of God; spirit of man or spirit of the enemy; unstable; cleansing; heart; desire for God – thirsting after Him; sea of humanity.
B. Calm – peace; still; sign of the presence of God; removal of threat; good sign – meaning God is in control.

The final thing deposited into my spirit was, "If we remain calm, our families will remain calm." This would apply across the board irrespective of where we presently find ourselves; i.e., married, single; widowed, etc.

Tying these symbols together, an evil spirit could be in a hidden, private place trying to entice us and strike fear into our hearts, so that we do not select the canoe on the beach to ultimately get into the calm waters and live at peace with one another irrespective of the storm we may be facing.

https://sheilaeismann.com/studying-prophetic-symbols/

Here are some additional factors to consider:

#1. The snake was flirting with its eyes. Risk is normally associated with enticement. When Adam and Eve entertained this, their lives were never the same nor was it so for anyone born after them.

The enemy of our souls or someone motivated by him can appear when and where we least expect him, catch us off guard, and attempt to seduce us.

This particular snake manifested in the bedroom, in a place where someone would normally feel safe and where many keep things they treasure.

Think about it, would you expect to find a snake in your closet? Probably only if you had pet snakes, and one of them happened to escape from its cage.

#2. It was a choice to select the canoe from the sandy beach, not mandatory. This is why the Apostle Paul used the wording he did in Romans 12:18. Peace should be our goal, but sometimes it's not within our control. Just imagine what it would look like if we did in fact choose to live peaceably and our actions followed our choice!

#3. Once we're inside the canoe or boat, we can invite Jesus and The Holy Spirit inside. I deem this is why there were no paddles initially seen in the vision. Calm is a sign of the presence of God. As irrational as it sounds, we can have perfect peace in the middle of a raging storm. It's all a matter of focus which is easier said than done.

Queries, please:

1. After pondering this prophetic vision, what are some suggestions you have to offer?
_____
_____
_____

2. How have you survived some of your most difficult crises and challenges?
_____
_____
_____

3. Do you know people who thrive on chaos? If so, how do you handle them or do you spend much time around them?
_____
_____
_____

4. What's your number one concern right now?
_____
_____
_____

5. Who's in your canoe with you?

_____

_____

_____

Our family is no different from any other. We've lost loved ones, received miracles and victories in several impossible situations, survived storms, and prefer to stay in the canoe in the calm waters as much as we possibly can.

The peace that surpasses understanding comes from keeping our eyes fixed upon Jesus Christ of Nazareth, the author and finisher of our faith, rather than the enticement. He reminded His disciples in John 14:27, "Peace I leave with you, My peace I give to you; not as the world gives do I give to you. Let not your heart be troubled, neither let it be afraid."

Please notice that the above verse indicates that it's Jesus' peace that He gives unto us which is supernatural. It can defy all logic, understanding, circumstances, situations, and everything else going on at the same time. It's totally different than the peace the world offers.

Perhaps you're in a place of total peace right now. Hallelujah! Please plan to spend some time in intercessory prayer as you lift others to the throne room of God and offer petitions on their behalf.

Prophetic Insights for Daily Living:

If applicable, command the coiled snake to permanently leave your closet as it's trying to compromise true peace and lure you into something else. Then take a walk to the sandy beach, select your canoe, and float into the gentle waters.

Enter the calm stream with Jesus and The Holy Spirit inside your canoe. They'll take the paddles and row for you. If storms are raging on the outside, trust Them with the outcome. After all, even the wind and the waves must obey Jesus! (Mark 4:35-41)

Here are a couple of scriptures upon which to meditate for this week:

Psalms 89:9 and 107:29-30.

In addition, Bible students, this would be a good prophetic exercise to increase your understanding.

Thank you, God, for giving us supernatural strength when we are weary, boundless hope when we are disappointed, and peace when we're anxious or stressed.

Sheila Eismann, Prophetic Seer, Blogger, Author & Teacher, publishes her weekly blog posts endeavoring to encourage others through God's word. Her writings include teaching and instructions on how to apply prophetic insights for daily living. You can subscribe to receive new blog posts on her website at www.sheilaeismann.com.

The Missing Piece
November 11, 2020
Prophetic Visions

People of all ages like puzzles of various sizes, shapes, and numbers of pieces. Are you one of them, and have you ever felt like your life's puzzle has a missing piece?

I have fond memories of my favorite aunt, Tante Anne, sitting at her card table working on jigsaw puzzles with enough pieces to virtually fill all the available space. The most amazing thing is that she did this with one eye as a result of a childhood accident. If there was a missing piece, she would scour around for days in search of it to complete the puzzle. Tante Anne was not content until she could stand back on her heels and stretch her 4-foot, 9-inch frame to gaze with sheer satisfaction upon one of her favorite pastimes.

The puzzle that manifested in the Spirit a couple of days ago had one missing piece. As I waited upon the Lord for further revelation, I saw the following word appear:

FAITH

The Holy Spirit impressed upon me that not everyone has this missing piece in their lives at the moment, however; some do, hence the prophetic vision.

According to dictionary.com, the definition of faith is as follows:

#1. confidence or trust in a person or thing: *faith in another's ability.*
#2. belief that is not based on proof: *He had faith that the hypothesis would be substantiated by fact.*
#3. belief in God or in the doctrines or teachings of religion: *the firm faith of the Pilgrims.*
#4. belief in anything, as a code of ethics, standards of merit, etc.: *to be of the same faith with someone concerning honesty.*
#5. a system of religious belief: *the Christian faith; the Jewish faith.*

#6. the obligation of loyalty or fidelity to a person, promise, engagement, etc.: *Failure to appear would be breaking faith.*

https://www.dictionary.com/browse/faith?s=t

For the sake of this week's blog post, I will be concentrating upon numbers #2 and #3 above.

One cannot even imagine how many sermons have been preached on faith over the past centuries. However, what's relevant for today is how this pertains to our own lives.

Some aspects to ponder, please:

Why do we even need faith?

_____

_____

_____

_____

After all, some people live their lives completely void of it. They adopt the attitude that whatever will be will be, so why worry about a single, solitary thing or try to exercise any kind of faith in a particular thing or person? This includes some who attend church regularly or at least they did pre-Covid 19. In Luke 17:5, "The apostles said to the Lord, 'Increase our faith!" Some would argue that this request only pertained to the original apostles, so since they are no longer living, there's no inherent right to ask for any increase. James

4:2 tells us that we do not have because we do not ask. Has God stopped answering prayers?

_____

_____

_____

According to Hebrews 11:1, "Now faith is the substance of things hoped for, the evidence of things not seen." Faith presents more of a challenge since it's not something tangible that you can see or reach out and touch. In addition, it's frustrating to look for unseen "evidence."

One of the things I appreciate most about God is that He leveled the playing field for people irrespective of the time frames in which they've been born. Under the Old Testament, faith in Him was the requirement for salvation which is necessary to save the sinner from sin. One example of this would be the patriarch of the Jewish and Christian faiths, Abraham. "And he (Abraham) believed in the LORD, and He accounted it to him for righteousness." (Genesis 15:6)

As New Testament believers, our rock-solid faith is in Jesus Christ of Nazareth, God's only begotten Son, Who died on the cross, was resurrected, and now sits at the right hand of the Father in heaven. (Mark 16:19; Romans 8:34; Ephesians 1:20; and Hebrews 10:11-14)

Without our intentional, expressed faith in Jesus Christ, we will not be able to enter heaven. During the years in which I taught children's Sunday School classes, this was commonly referred to as *The Roman Road to*

Salvation based upon Romans 10:9-10, "that if you confess with your mouth the Lord Jesus and believe in your heart that God has raised Him from the dead, you will be saved. For with the heart one believes unto righteousness, and with the mouth confession is made unto salvation."

Most spiritual contentions regarding salvation stem from the deity of Jesus Christ. False christs have been around since Jesus' day. (Matthew 24:5, 23-25)

This is why it's paramount to ascertain what your church or religious organization is teaching and espousing regarding the same. Who is your Jesus?

_____
_____
_____

Cults purport and claim a different Jesus. The reason this is important is that it's faith in the real Jesus of the actual Bible Who can save our life when it's all over. Have you placed your faith in Him? It's never too late to do so. If you've strayed far from Him, ask for forgiveness, and run into His everlasting arms. He's waiting for you!

Staying on track with the original prophetic vision, after spending time in prayer with the Lord and waiting for further instruction, I sensed the following:

The missing puzzle piece doesn't pertain to basic faith in Jesus Christ. Rather, this faith is being tested. Do we have faith to trust God in ALL circumstances? _____

Prophetic symbolisms for puzzles are confusion; test; riddle or parable; or searching out mysteries and enigmas.

It's by faith that we endure until the end of whatever trial or struggle we're facing.

Hebrews 11:6, "But without faith *it is* impossible to please *Him,* for he who comes to God must believe that He is, and *that* He is a rewarder of those who diligently seek Him." In times that our faith is being tested, we must seek God.

I have a poem tacked to my bulletin board titled,

"Faith Is

Faith is risking what is for what is yet to be.

It is taking small steps knowing they lead to bigger ones.

Faith is holding on when you want to let go.

It is letting go when you want to hold on.

Faith is saying yes when everything else says no.

It is believing all things are possible in the midst of impossibilities.

Faith is looking beyond what is and trusting what will be.

It is the presence of light in darkness, the presence of God in all."

(Ellen M. Cuomo)

Faith is needed to complete the puzzle whether it's a profession for the first time or retrieving lost faith and exercising it. Maybe it's time to visit the spice cabinet and look for a mustard seed! (Matthew 17:20)

Today we honor our Veterans and active military personnel. It could be that some of them need their faith boosted as well. Please plan to do something extra special, kind, and unexpected for one of them who may have a missing piece to his or her puzzle. Actually, the gift of an actual puzzle might be just the ticket! Another suggestion would be my husband's book titled *Freedom Is Your Destiny!* which chronicles his back-to-back tours of duty in Vietnam.

https://sheilaeismann.com/product/freedom-is-your-destiny/

Prophetic Insights for Daily Living:

Let us continue to walk by faith and not by sight as we complete life's puzzle with all of its pieces.

A final word of encouragement: If you feel like you've misplaced your faith or it's missing, pray and ask the Lord to help you find it again.

I've prayed this prayer many times over the years when I've misplaced something, and the Lord has been so faithful to reveal the whereabouts of exactly what I've been searching for: "There is nothing hidden that won't be revealed, and there is nothing secret that won't become known and come to light." (Luke 8:17 ISV)

Also, Luke 15:8-9, "Or suppose a woman has ten silver coins and loses one. Doesn't she light a lamp, sweep the house and search carefully until she finds it? And when she finds it, she calls her friends and neighbors together and says, 'Rejoice with me; I have found my lost coin.'"

So, whether it's a lost puzzle piece, coin, faith, or whatever it may be, God knows exactly where it is. He's just waiting for your call. (Jeremiah 33:3)

We may not know what the message is when the picture or situation is incomplete, but we must have faith in God, and trust Him. It will become clear when the missing piece is found!

Sheila Eismann, Prophetic Seer, Blogger, Author & Teacher, publishes her weekly blog posts endeavoring to encourage others through God's word. Her writings include teaching and instructions on how to apply prophetic insights for daily living. You can subscribe to receive new blog posts on her website at www.sheilaeismann.com.

SOL: Spirit of Lawlessness

November 17, 2020
Prophetic Teachings

Having been raised on Sage Creek Farms which included sweet cherry, pie cherry, and prune orchards, I didn't expect to find peaches, pears, or apples at harvest time. At first blush, what could this possibly have to do with the spirit of lawlessness?

It's often been said that you can't judge a book by its cover, but during Jesus' Sermon on the Mount, He aptly instructed His disciples to look for fruit.

Jesus states in Matthew 7:15-20, "Beware of false prophets, who come to you in sheep's clothing, but inwardly they are ravenous wolves. You will know them by their fruits. Do men gather grapes from thornbushes or figs from thistles? Even so, every good tree bears good fruit, but a bad tree bears bad fruit. A good tree cannot bear bad fruit, nor *can* a bad tree bear good fruit. Every tree that does not bear good fruit is cut down and thrown into the fire. Therefore by their fruits you will know them."

If you continue to read this passage of scripture down through verse 23, there's also a stern warning to those who practice lawlessness.

The Greek word for lawlessness in this instance is *anomia* (Strong's G458) and means "the condition of one without law – either because ignorant of it, or because violating it; contempt and violation of law, iniquity, or wickedness."

https://www.blueletterbible.org/lang/Lexicon/Lexicon.cfm?strongs=G458&t=KJV

Suffice it to say, it's not just physical trees that bear fruit, but people, institutions, countries, and so forth.

Some would argue that we're never to judge because, with the same judgment with which we judge, the same will be applied to us. (Matthew 7:1-2) This restriction neither implies nor infers that a disciple of Jesus should never judge.

We are to make a righteous judgment, completely void of fault-finding and criticism, to follow Jesus and obey His commands. If we don't make a judgment and look at the fruit of something, how can we ever discern whether it is good or bad, helpful or detrimental?

Prophetic symbolisms for the law are as follows:

The Old Testament
Moses' writings
Law of sin and death
Law sheds light on sin
Word of God
Legalism

Law of faith

Law written on our hearts

Liberty/Freedom

Our civil and criminal legal systems

Law of the Spirit of Life

If we plug in the opposites of the above-list, we can garner a better idea of lawlessness or something which is void of the law. A couple of examples would be no sin and (spiritual) death or no liberty and freedom.

When we boil it down, the root of all lawlessness is rebellion which is one of the manifestations of the perverse spirit. (Isaiah 19:14). The Hebrew word for perverse in this scripture is *'av 'eh* (Strong's H5773) which means distorting, perverting, warping.

https://www.blueletterbible.org/lang/Lexicon/Lexicon.cfm?strongs=H5773&t=KJV

The 19th chapter of Isaiah describes God's judgment upon Egypt which is symbolic of the world; slavery to Pharaoh; worldliness; bondage; and idolatry.

Other manifestations of the perverse spirit include any manner of perversion, lovers of self, false teachers, hate, error, snares, etc.

Lawlessness is breaking the law, whether it's God's moral laws or the ones instituted by civil authorities.

Followers of Jesus hate the deeds or fruits of lawlessness. We are to be law-abiding Christians according to Romans 13:1-7 and 1 Peter 2:13-17 unless the laws instituted by man contradict God's laws. (Acts 5:29)

What happens to a nation when righteous laws are ignored or broken? Lawlessness, chaos, and extreme loss are the results. Laws are required in human governments to maintain decency, order, righteousness, and protect life.

https://sheilaeismann.com/three-spiritual-clues/

A stellar Old Testament example of this would be what transpired during the cycle of the various judges. It's painful and discouraging to read through the book of Judges. It chronicles a period of steep decline with each emerging instance of disobedience and sin leaving Israel even further from God with disastrous consequences. The greater degree of disobedience required a more severe punishment by Israel's enemies. A common mantra of the day was, "In those days Israel had no king; everyone did as they saw fit." (Judges 21:25) Doing what is right in one's own eyes is lawlessness. Proverbs 21:2 informs us, "Every way of a man is right in his own eyes, but the LORD weighs the hearts."

This is not to infer that there weren't some good and God-fearing judges who served during their time, but with increased cycles of lawlessness, Israel finally came off the rails and was forced into captivity. I can only imagine if we could go back in history and interview one of the people in Assyria or Babylon and ask him if it would have been better for Israel to have collectively obeyed God and His laws rather than disregard them. Speaking of captivity, consider the fruits of that!

Acts 19 portrays lawlessness in the New Testament with a definite "follow the crowd mentality." In Ephesus, the Apostle Paul was introducing people to the truth of Jesus Christ and the good news of the gospel. This caused sales of the silver shrines of the fertility goddess, Diana, to plummet which was not the least bit insignificant.

The entire city was filled with wrath and confusion as the Ephesians rushed into the 25,000-seat amphitheater. The entire assembly was confused, and most of them did not know why they'd come together. Once the clerk could control the crowd and quiet them down, he urged them to pursue the proper legal channels which were in place at the time. (Acts 19:21-41)

Verse 40 states, "For we are in danger of being called in question for today's uproar, there being no reason which we may give to account for this disorderly gathering." The danger was that it could have brought the heavy-handed discipline of Rome upon the city of Ephesus.

Historically speaking, the peace that the Roman Empire brought to that part of the world was important to Rome. They enforced severe discipline for unruly cities and people groups. They had zero tolerance for any kind of rebellion or rioting. The city of Ephesus had to ask itself, "Do we want our own freedom or do we run the risk of being ruled by the Roman army?"

Spirits work through people, but a door has to be opened to grant them entry. Once this door is opened, and if it's not quickly shut, much havoc can be wreaked in short order. A "magnet principle" comes into play wherein one foul spirit will quickly invite many others to join it. Before long, it can become a legion. (Matthew 8:28-34)

In some instances, it can take time before spirits leave their significant mark, but this does not seem to be the case with lawlessness. One explanation for this could be that since we are born with a sinful nature, the situation isn't remedied until we give our lives to Jesus Christ and He becomes Lord over them. (Genesis 6:5 and 8:21; Psalm 51:5; Ephesians 2:3; Romans 3:23 and 5:12)

Prophetic Insights for Daily Living:

Fast forward to a modern-day application, and I would earnestly encourage you to write down your answers to the following questions:

#1. Have you witnessed or heard of the deeds of the spirit of lawlessness at work?

_____
_____
_____

#2. If so, could you list some examples?

#3. What is the fruit or the result of this spirit?

#4. Are any of the fruits good or positive?

#5. What do you think opened the door(s) to unleash this spirit in the first place?

#6. What are the dangers of this spirit at work?

#7. What is the overall effect of this spirit on our nation at this time?

#8. What remedies do you deem need to be instituted to rid our land of the spirit of lawlessness?

#9. If the spirit isn't dealt with properly and lawfully, how does our future look?

#10. What could you as one individual do to make a difference to ensure a God-fearing, law-abiding society?

Here's sort of another aspect to throw into our modern-day mix:

Postmodernism is the rejection of objective or absolute truth. To a postmodernist, truth is subjective, including moral truth. People can't know anything with certainty. Each person decides for himself or herself what is true, including what is morally true, and each person's truth can change over time. Because there is no objective truth, one person's truth is just as valid as another person's truth. If a postmodernist claims to be a Christian, God is what that person wants Him (or Her) to be, as is the manner of salvation.

Postmodernists reject the authority of the dominant group in society and assert that all ethnic, cultural, racial, and religious groups have the right to their own truth that is just as valid as the truth of the dominant group. Postmodernism became the philosophy of the identity politics movement.

King Jesus, His kingdom, dominion, and authority will ultimately prevail. It will take supreme strength, wisdom, and courage to navigate the days ahead which could be likened to the picture below for which our state is famous.

May the peace of God rule and reign in our hearts as we keep our eyes on Jesus Christ, the Author and Finisher of our faith. (Hebrews 12:2) Please make sure He's in your kayak or boat with you!

Sheila Eismann, Prophetic Seer, Blogger, Author & Teacher, publishes her weekly blog posts endeavoring to encourage others through God's word. Her writings include teaching and instructions on how to apply prophetic insights for daily living. You can subscribe to receive new blog posts on her website at www.sheilaeismann.com.

Give Thanks
November 24, 2020
Holidays

In light of the humdinger year we've had, are you finding it hard to give thanks **in** everything much less for anything? Please notice I didn't suggest giving thanks **for** everything. Oh my, what a difference a small but powerful preposition can make!

When writing to the church at Thessalonica, the Apostle Paul instructed the following in 1 Thessalonians 5:16-18,

"Rejoice always, pray without ceasing, in everything give thanks; for this is the will of God in Christ Jesus for you."

Say whaaaaaat? Is it actually God's will for us to give thanks in all circumstances despite the loss, hardship, trial, tribulation, and persecution? Surely you jest! I can just hear some of you howling through clenched teeth as you read this and reply, "You have no clue what 2020 has dished up for me and my family."

Suffice it to say, I've not heard of or personally spoken to anyone who's testified that this year has been a cake walk, picnic in the park, or life on Easy Street.

By way of a brief history and background regarding the church at Thessalonica, the Apostle Paul and Prophet Silas made a brief stop there on Paul's second missionary journey. They found it to be a very hostile environment for preaching the gospel which resulted in an early departure from the city. Ergo, Paul dispatched Timothy to the city to further establish and encourage the Christians there. He instructed them to persevere in the faith despite what was going on around them. That's sage advice for us today.

The Thessalonica situation occurred in a geographic region that was an important port city and thriving commercial area located in the northwest corner of the Aegean Sea. The travel routes made it one of the most strategic cities and trade centers of the entire Roman Empire. With a population of approximately 200,000 and the largest city of the Macedonian province, we're not talking about some wide spot in the road or 500 miles out in the ding weeds where they have to pipe daylight into you. The Apostle Paul's original intent, with the help of The Holy Spirit, was to spread the gospel throughout Macedonia and Greece. (Acts 16:9-10)

After hastily leaving Macedonia, Paul and Silas's opponents chased after them to Berea and continued to harass them. (Acts 16:35-17:15). Perhaps you've experienced something similar in that someone tried to chase you out of town as well or bring similar harassment.

It's at this juncture where all of us have a choice based upon some considerations. Please feel free to personalize this brief list.

1. Irrespective of what's going on, there will always be persecution in one form or another. Sometimes it will be blatant while at other times it will be covert. One day it will seem to be wearing one dress or outfit and a completely different one the next. Camouflage can be challenging, slithering, and sneaky.
2. If we'll allow it, tremendous personal and spiritual growth takes place during this time.
3. Character is formed in the crucible. Has this ever happened to you, and if so, in what manner?

_____
_____
_____
_____

4. When we suffer together, what does it produce?
_____

5. There's an opportunity for the fruit of the Spirit to develop within us. "But the fruit of the Spirit is love, joy, peace, longsuffering, goodness, faithfulness, gentleness, self-control. Against such there is no law." (Galatians 5:22-23)

6. Speaking of the law, which in the Galatians' case was a reference to the Old Testament law delivered on Mount Sinai (Exodus 20:20), have you witnessed or experienced strange enforcements or enactments of civil law in your geographic region during this year?

7. This may be the most challenging season yet to yield to The Holy Spirit to allow for the growth of our spirits, especially that of self-control and longsuffering.

8. It takes a lot of maturity to come to grips with the fact that it's God's will for us to give thanks in every circumstance. Why do you think that is?

9. The seeds of bitterness and resentment aren't usually found in the soil of a thankful heart. Each time we choose to give thanks, it's as if a supernatural spade continues to turn the heart soil and keep it soft, watered, and nurtured.

Holidays are synonymous with comfort and joy.

https://sheilaeismann.com/christmas-themes/

When talking to a family member recently, we came to the mutual conclusion of how important it is to hear the voice of a loved one, especially if we can't be together around the Thanksgiving table. In addition, our typical "feast" may look a little different or less this time around.

Prophetic Insights for Daily Living:

#1. Perhaps a "feast of the heart and spirit" will bring more comfort and joy than a "feast around the table."

#2. Spiritual food will sustain us long after physical food has been consumed.

#3. Between November 26th and December 26th, fill a jar or bowl with 30 ideas or one-liners for which you can give thanks. Plan to draw one out each day. It's amazing what a simple, practical act or declaration can contribute to our overall attitudes and actions. These can be very elementary or action-oriented if you like. Invite your children or other family members to participate.

#4. Sometimes it helps to place our focus upon others rather than upon ourselves.

#5. You'll feel so much better and your "self-barometer" will soar when you do something kind for someone, especially when they have no way to repay you or enhance your life.

#6. Gratitude is an attitude. Do we need an AA – Attitude Adjustment?

#7. Choose one good memory daily and focus intently upon it. After all, these belong to you, and no one can take them from you. They will help to strengthen you and bring contentment to your heart.

A popular phrase that has been bandied about this year is "the new normal." Do you think the Apostle Paul would have used this verbiage during his shipwrecks, beatings, imprisonment, abasements, periods of lack, and attacks? Why or why not? Come to think of it, there really wasn't much normal about his life after his encounter with the Lord Jesus Christ on the Damascus Road. (Acts 9:3-9)

In His omnipotence, God chose this particular apostle to pen two-thirds of the New Testament. In light of Paul's life before his conversion, one might not consider him to be a prime candidate to be used as such a sovereign instrument. (Acts 22:1-5; 26:9-11; and 1 Corinthians 15:9)

The Apostle Paul yielded to God's choice, fought the good fight of faith, and gave thanks in all circumstances. The end result was the reward of the crown of eternal life to be awarded to him. (2 Timothy 4:7-8)

It would appear that it's high time to cowgirl up, cowboy up, or whatever up we decide, so we can give thanks in everything!

Here's wishing you a peaceful Thanksgiving. All of us have so much for which to be thankful.

Sheila Eismann, Prophetic Seer, Blogger, Author & Teacher, publishes her weekly blog posts endeavoring to encourage others through God's word. Her writings include teaching and instructions on how to apply prophetic insights for daily living. You can subscribe to receive new blog posts on her website at www.sheilaeismann.com.

The Hand, The Keys, and The Bridge

December 1, 2020
Prophetic Visions

A vision was given to me a couple of weeks ago wherein I saw a woman holding a key ring on her forefinger. I did not see any part of her other than her left hand. She did not speak. There was nothing and no one else around. As you read this blog, please pay attention as to whether or not it could pertain to the election results.

On the key ring were two, new, identical silver-colored house keys and an older vehicle key which was shaped like a Toyota® car key.

My eyes were drawn first to the house keys rather than the car key, which was a bit longer.

Behind the woman was a wooden bridge in a rural, peaceful setting with some foliage in the background. The accompanying picture to this blog does not feature a wooden bridge; however, this photo is used for illustrative purposes.

I waited upon The Holy Spirit for several days to see if there was anything He wanted to add to this vision. I've now felt the release to include it with my weekly blog posts.

Let's break down the elements of this vision, shall we?

#1. Cars

(a) Cars can symbolize our lives, families, churches, businesses, ministries, and so forth.

(b) The uniqueness or specifics of a Toyota car key are included in the following:

"Design Elements of the Toyota Logo

"The Toyota logo may appear relatively simplistic at first glance; however, it contains several exciting and unique design elements. To see the meaning behind the Toyota logo, one need look no further than Toyota's own explanation:

"The two perpendicular ovals inside the larger oval represent the heart of the customer and the heart of the company. They are overlapped to represent a mutually beneficial relationship and trust between each other. The overlapping of the two perpendicular ovals inside the outer oval symbolizes "T" for Toyota, as well as a steering wheel, representing the vehicle itself. The outer oval symbolizes the world embracing Toyota. Each oval is contoured with different stroke thicknesses, similar to the "brush" art known in Japanese culture."

https://blog.logomyway.com/history-toyota-logo/

(c) In the above explanation, there's a distinct emphasis upon the word oval or oval design.

"**O'VAL**, *adjective* [Latin ovum, an egg.]
1. Of the shape or figure of an egg; oblong; curvilinear; resembling the longitudinal section of an egg. It is sometimes synonymous with elliptical, but an ellipsis is equally broad at both ends, and is not strictly egg-shaped.
2. Pertaining to eggs; done in the egg; as *oval* conceptions.
O'VAL, *noun* A body or figure in the shape of an egg.
http://www.kingjamesbibledictionary.com/Dictionary/oval

Eggs symbolize promises; new beginnings; gifts; schemes or plans; potential or **fertility**.

"Toyota is a variation of the name Toyoda. The original Toyoda company invented and produced numerous types of looms. In 1933, Toyoda decided to foray into the automotive market, expanding greatly in 1956 after steady successes. Toyoda means "**fertile** rice patty" referring to Japan's most prominent cash crop." (**fertility/fertile** – emphases mine)

https://www.google.com/search?q=toyota+logos&oq=toyota+logos&aqs=chrome..69i57j0j0i10l6.2180j0j7&sourceid=chrome&ie=UTF-8

#2. Keys

Keys are symbolic of authority; wisdom; knowledge; understanding; ability; important or indispensable; Jesus Christ; opportunity; access; control; the way out of something; heart; God's will in a situation; love; revelation; prophecy; faith; prayer; unity; and doors.

These keys were made of silver which represents knowledge; knowledge of God; redemption; idolatry; spiritual adultery; or redemption money. Also, there's no silver in heaven – only gold is mentioned. (Revelation 21:18-21)

In addition, the keys could have appeared in any fashion in the vision, but these were dangling from a woman's left forefinger.

Fingers indicate feeling; sensitivity; discerning; conviction; works; direction; looking for evidence through feelings; or amplification in intricacy and detail of what is being done, whether with good or evil intent.

#3. Hand

A hand represents words; deeds (good or evil); labor; service; idolatry; spiritual warfare; strength; power; action; possession; one person's side of the agreement; heart; flesh; works; the church – God's hands; God's provision or power; dominion; control; authority; responsibility; pledge or oath; opposition; assistance; carrying; grabbing something; giving or a gift;

payment; hit, hurt or doing harm; available – at the ready; within reach or grasp; capture or custody; invitation; direction; or hidden.

Left (Hand) is symbolized by spiritual; spiritual change; man's weakness; God's strength or ability demonstrated through man's weakness; rejection; weakness in general; flesh; unbelief; cursed; death; judgment; heart; foolishness; carefree lifestyle; or soulish matters.

#4. House

Symbolisms for a house are person or family; individual; church; a dwelling place; home; heart; identity; roots; covering; ministry; or business.

#5. Bridge

A bridge is symbolized by support or way; faith; trial of faith; joined; church; means to an end; life's passage or journey; the cross; Jesus Christ; relationship or communication; or human-made structure.

The bridge in the vision was made of wood which is symbolic of temporary; the flesh; humanity; carnal reasoning; lust; or spiritual building material. All bridges are man-made.

There's a warning in 1 Corinthians 3:12 to Christians to not build upon the foundation of wood which is carnal reasoning and coming from self rather than the Spirit of God. We are to build upon gold (wisdom), silver (knowledge), and precious stones (the witness of God's word).

In looking at the prophetic symbolisms for the various objects in the vision, there's some overlapping which could be interpreted as reinforcement or emphasis.

#6. The number 2

There are 2 house keys.

Symbolisms for the number 2 are union (two becoming one flesh – Mark 10:6-8); division; separation; witnessing; difference; association or agreement; reward or multiplication; double-mindedness; repetitive situation; twins; or death as it precedes the number three which represents resurrection.

#7. The number 3

There are 3 keys; 3 ovals of the Toyota logo; and 3 cut-outs in the house keys.

3 symbolizes the Trinity; triune man – body, soul and spirit; separation of flesh and spirit; complete; resurrection; or third heaven.

Prophetic Insights for Daily Living:

A. This vision could pertain to the November 3rd, 2020 election results.

B. There are four 3's to consider: national election results on the 3rd; 3 keys; 3 cut-outs on the keys; and 3 ovals of the Toyota logo.

C. The two-house keys are new, and there are two governmental houses with newly elected members; i.e., the U. S. Senate and U. S. House of Representatives. The two "inner ovals" of the Toyota logo are at cross purposes of one another. That could be said oftentimes of both houses of Congress and not just following the most recent election.

D. The outer circle of the Toyota logo represents the steering wheel of the vehicle. One cannot drive a car without a key. In the vision, the car key was much older than the house keys which could indicate much more experience.

E. Who owns the car?_____

F. Who's in the driver's seat?_____

G. Ovals are shaped like eggs which can represent schemes, plans or fertility. What fertile schemes are being hatched an/or implemented?
_____

H. The two perpendicular ovals inside the larger oval (of the Toyota logo) symbolize the heart of the customer and the heart of the company. They are overlapped to represent a mutually beneficial relationship and trust between each other. We must ask ourselves, "Is there a mutually beneficial relationship and trust in one another and in our nation right now?"_____
_____

I. The bridge is in the background. There's no way to know for sure whether the person holding the keys is on a road to the bridge, but what comes to me is that we will cross that bridge when we have to or if we have to. That saying is usually implemented when a major decision may have to be made when someone doesn't want to make it right now.

J. The woman, whose left hand was shaped like a cocked handgun in the vision, could be holding the all-important keys to a "smoking gun" of some sort.

https://sheilaeismann.com/studying-prophetic-symbols/

I would earnestly and sincerely invite you to pray into this vision as well as others you may have received. If you have any revelation, I would appreciate you posting it as a comment at the end of this blog post or sending it to me via email: sheila@sheilaeismann.com

For Bible and/or prophecy students a fun exercise would be to print this blog post and focus upon the overlapping or duplication of the symbolisms which might lend some clues to the overall interpretation.

Granted, this one is a real "headscratcher," so to speak; however, "*It is* the glory of God to conceal a matter, but the glory of kings *is* to search out a matter. (Proverbs 25:2)

Keep a sharp eye on this vision to see what the future brings. Since we are kings and priests under the New Covenant in the New Testament, let us begin the search and treasure hunt! (1 Peter 2:5; Revelation 1:6; 5:10)

As you're studying this workbook, how does this vision speak to you in light of the fact that a lot has happened since the November 2020 election?

_____
_____
_____

Sheila Eismann, Prophetic Seer, Blogger, Author & Teacher, publishes her weekly blog posts endeavoring to encourage others through God's word. Her writings include teaching and instructions on how to apply prophetic insights for daily living. You can subscribe to receive new blog posts on her website at www.sheilaeismann.com.

Prophetic Insights For Daily Living – Volume 1

The Frozen Footprint

December 9, 2020
Prophetic Visions

What do you enjoy most about winter and Christmas? Is it decorating sugar cookies with your kiddos or grandkiddos or the traditional carols are sung outside since we're still amid the pandemic? Speaking of braving the cold, this week's message pertains to a prophetic vision to seek the lost featuring the frozen footprint, a lantern, and a Christmas tree.

When the vision opened, I held an old-fashioned lantern in my right hand as I approached a Christmas tree decorated with multi-colored lights located on the outskirts of a town. I looked down at the ground and saw a frozen footprint in the snow. I knew by revelation this was a man's right shoe footprint who would have been wearing about a size 10 boot. This must have been made when the snow was fresh because you could clearly see the outline of it. My attention was drawn to the lone footprint as the left one was about 18 inches from the right one. (The image accompanying this blog post features several footprints, but this is the closest picture I could find to portray the overall message.)

Darkness and nightfall were fast approaching in this country setting. There were no gifts under the tree or empty boxes wrapped with Christmas paper which are found in some outdoor displays.

In the next scene of the vision, I saw others following behind me carrying identical antique lanterns. They were about 8-10 feet apart, moving slowly and searching the landscape.

As I glanced over my shoulder to the right, I recognized one person behind me whose first name is Sharon. Her name means *Princess* with the accompanying lifetime scripture verse:

"But you *are* a chosen generation, a royal priesthood, a holy nation, His own special people, that you may proclaim the praises of Him who called you out of darkness into His marvelous light;" (1 Peter 2:9)

I received this vision on the 5th day of December 2020. Five is symbolic of God's grace to man; man's responsibility; redemption; favor; and abundance. The scripture that was impressed upon me was from John 9:4-5, "I (Jesus) must work the works of Him who sent Me while it is day; *the* night is coming when no one can work. As long as I am in the world, I am the light of the world."

As Jesus' disciples, we must work while it is still day as night is fast approaching.

This is not to be confused with works-based salvation which is one of the hallmarks of a cult. It teaches that Jesus' atoning death on the cross is insufficient for total salvation. Another significant clue is that a bunch of works is added to their false gospel which is one of the chief ways to control their members. They intentionally misappropriate James 2:17, "Thus also faith by itself, if it does not have works, is dead."

The Bible helps us to understand salvation through Christ alone. Ephesians 2:8-9, "For by grace you have been saved through faith, and that not of yourselves; *it is* the gift of God, **not of works**, lest anyone should boast." (Emphasis mine)

Yes, we are to work within God's kingdom with the individual and corporate assignments He has given to us, but these are not to be confused with the basic requirement for salvation.

I deem the main theme of this vision is searching for the lost which could pertain to those who once knew Christ as their personal Lord and Savior and have walked away from Him or have never been introduced to the real Jesus of the Bible. There's another important distinction here as the cults have their own version of who Jesus is.

Since there are only 16 days left until Christmas, I am treating this as a **NOW** word or a word in due season. (Proverbs 15:23)

It's not always going to be convenient to search for the lost. If we revisit when the vision first opened in the Spirit realm, it was cold outside, and darkness was fast approaching. Time is of the essence.

The vision does not explicitly state what the man who left the footprints was doing, but he was obviously drawn to the lights.

Interestingly, each of the people in the vision was carrying antique-looking lanterns as opposed to modern-day flashlights or using the same on their cell phones.

I knew by revelation these were heavenly issued lanterns which symbolize God's word; the believer's heart; a church; The Spirit of God; and truth.

The Spirit zoomed in to where I could see just the words "**Psalm 36:9**" painted vertically down one side of the lantern, and each person's first name was painted with blue Calligraphy font down the other side. This verse from the 36th Psalm reads, "For with You *is* the fountain of life; In Your light we see light." Blue is the color of heaven.

In John 8:12 we read, "Then Jesus spoke to them again, saying, 'I am the light of the world. He who follows Me shall not walk in darkness, but have the light of life.'"

Also, "And the light shines in the darkness, and the darkness did not comprehend it." (John 1:5)

It's incumbent upon us to help others come to the true light which is Jesus Christ of Nazareth.

There was obviously a candle inside each lantern that burned. This would not shed much light, but this is what the vision contained. Using an ancient lantern would mean that the searchers would have to be close to the person to find him. The lanterns would not light up what is far away. It would have to be a one-on-one interaction.

Plugging in some other symbolism and Bible verses help us to continue to pray into this vision:

1. It was winter outside which is representative of death; hardship or tribulation; little light (no revelation of Jesus Christ); progress with difficulty; time of hibernation or rest; time of pruning; unbelief.

2. Snow covered the landscape which indicates a time of refreshing; God's word; or timely message. What could be timelier than the salvation message? (Romans 10:9-10)

3. Evergreen (Christmas) tree with multi-colored lights is symbolic of feeding on the Word of God daily and long life. The way to have everlasting life is through belief in Jesus Christ, God's one and only begotten Son. (John 3:16)

4. The sole print of the boot most likely pertains to the souls of men. It's sort of a play on words. Boots speak of an external or outward walk; work; or arduous path.

5. A footprint in and of itself points to steps of faith; claiming of spiritual inheritance; angelic evidence; or evidence of strongholds. The right (footprint) signifies strength; faith; preferred, preeminence, above, before or double portion; authority; longevity; wisdom; future destiny; and the spiritual realm.

6. An antique lantern speaks of the old, antique, or ancient ways. Jeremiah 6:16 comes to mind:

"Thus says the Lord:

"Stand in the ways and see,
And ask for the old paths, where the good way *is,*
And walk in it;
Then you will find rest for your souls.
But they (Israel) said, 'We will not walk *in it.*'"

Additional Bible verses to ponder in light of the overall prophetic vision:

Psalm 119:105

Proverbs 20:27

John 11:9

Encouragement to seek the lost comes from Luke 15:1-7 which tells us the parable of the lost sheep.

"Then all the tax collectors and the sinners drew near to Him (Jesus) to hear Him. And the Pharisees and scribes complained, saying, 'This Man receives sinners and eats with them.' So He spoke this parable to them, saying:

"What man of you, having a hundred sheep, if he loses one of them, does not leave the ninety-nine in the wilderness, and go after the one which is lost until he finds it? And when he has found *it,* he lays *it* on his shoulders, rejoicing. And when he comes home, he calls together *his* friends and neighbors, saying to them, 'Rejoice with me, for I have found my sheep which was lost!' I say to you that likewise there will be more joy in heaven over one sinner who repents than over ninety-nine just persons who need no repentance."

A consideration: this prophetic vision is in conjunction with the timing of the Feast of Dedication or Hanukkah.

The events of this prophetic vision take place in the winter which mirrors the timing of *Hanukkah*. In addition, it's called the Feast of Dedication. In Biblical times, this took place in Jerusalem. (John 10:22) It celebrates the rededication of the Jewish temple in December 164 B.C. after its desecration by the Seleucid ruler Antiochus Epiphanes IV in 167.

Hanukkah, also called **Chanukah**, occurs on December 10–18, 2020 (Jewish Year 5781) this year.

Each Christian is a temple of the Holy Spirit (1 Corinthians 6:19), and all Christians grow into a holy temple in the Lord. You also are being built together for a dwelling place of God in the Spirit. (Ephesians 2:21–22)

Although Christians celebrate December 25th as the day of Jesus's birth, He was born in the spring. December 25th may be the day of his conception.

Prophetic Insights for Daily Living:

In this season, who's the one that the One (Jesus) is laying upon your heart to seek?

_____
_____
_____

Proverbs 6:23, "For the commandment *is* a lamp,
And the law a light; Reproofs of instruction *are* the way of life,"

Some would incorrectly opine that we are no longer under the commandments and law of God. Jesus came to fulfill all the law and the prophets as He instructed His disciples on the Sermon on the Mount in Matthew 5:17, "Do not think that I came to destroy the Law or the Prophets. I did not come to destroy but to fulfill."

The person in the prophetic vision was drawn to the multi-colored lights on the Christmas tree which did not satisfy him. Only the true light of the world, Jesus Christ, can do that.

Jesus is the reason for the season. All of the other glitz and glamor pale in significance to Him, and the sole purpose He came to earth was to save sinners. Time is running so short to share His message of love, forgiveness, and hope.

Even if you don't have an antique lantern on hand, God will show you by and through the power of His Son and His Holy Spirit what method to use to search for the lost person. Believers spiritually are each a member of the body of Christ because He works through each of us to accomplish what He desires. (1 Corinthians 12:12-14; 26-27)

Are you willing to sacrifice the comforts of warmth (people were outside in the frigid cold searching with lanterns in the vision), your time, and plans to help someone enter the kingdom of heaven before it's too late?

_____

_____

This is a priority that won't be convenient or comfortable unless you like to spend lots of time in cold, snowy weather! What other priorities would you add to this prophetic vision?

_____

_____

_____

Each of us only has so many days ordained in which to fulfill his or her destiny. (Psalm 139:16) May we use them wisely as we continue to shine as bright lights in the world. (Philippians 2:14-16)

https://sheilaeismann.com/spiritual-time/

Please join me in praying for the lost:

Father, we thank You that You sent Your Son to seek and save those who are lost. (Luke 19:10) Each of us is made in Your image, and You desire that none perish but come to everlasting life. (2 Peter 3:9) We know that time is of the essence to spread the true gospel of Jesus Christ. Please show us our individual assignments as to whom to search for and share the good news as we know that You'll have gone ahead of us to prepare their heart soil to receive it. In Jesus' name, we pray, Amen.

Sheila Eismann, Prophetic Seer, Blogger, Author & Teacher, publishes her weekly blog posts endeavoring to encourage others through God's word. Her writings include teaching and instructions on how to apply prophetic insights for daily living. You can subscribe to receive new blog posts on her website at www.sheilaeismann.com.

Kindness ~~ An Invaluable Currency

December 16, 2020
Encouragement

Do you deem heaven may have its own kind of spiritual currency? There are innumerable types of worldly ones, of course, but have you ever considered that any of them would be labeled an invaluable currency?

We normally associate monetary forms with any of the following:

"*noun, plural* **cur·ren·cies.**

1. something that is used as a medium of exchange; money.

2. general acceptance; prevalence; vogue.

3. a time or period during which something is widely accepted and circulated.

4. the fact or quality of being widely accepted and circulated from person to person.

5. circulation, as of coin."

https://www.dictionary.com/browse/currency?s=thttps://www.dictionary.com/browse/currency?s=t

With the all-important adjective ***invaluable*** preceding the noun ***currency***, invaluable pertains to the price of something which is beyond calculation regarding value or worth. In other words, it's priceless.

The Greek word for kindness is *chrestotes* (Strong's G5544) which means "usefulness; i.e., morally, excellence (in character or demeanor): – gentleness, good(-ness), kindness."

https://www.blueletterbible.org/lang/Lexicon/Lexicon.cfm?strongs=G5544&t=KJVhttps://www.blueletterbible.org/lang/Lexicon/Lexicon.cfm?strongs=G5544&t=KJV

What if we desire to do something kind for someone, but have no extra money, goods, or time?

If we're unable to do something tangible for someone, at least we can speak a kind word. These remain as jewels in the heart long after which they are spoken. This is especially important for people whose love language is words of affirmation.

The Bible contains several important verses regarding the theme of this blog post. Here are some if you would like to do a little topical study of your own:

1 Corinthians 13:4
Acts 28:2
Ephesians 2:7
Colossians 3:12
2 Peter 1:7

After looking these up, which one(s) speak to you and why?_____

_____

_____

_____

_____

In approximately A.D. 63, the Apostle Paul penned an epistle to Titus, one of his converts, who lived on the island of Crete which is located about 100 miles southeast of Greece.

To the Cretan's credit, they developed a somewhat prosperous trading economy and booming business center due primarily to their agricultural efforts. Exorbitant excesses were one unfortunate result of this. In addition, sometimes when there's no lack of material goods and success, one's spiritual life isn't considered a high priority.

The small Christian church in Crete lacked sound leadership, and the false teachers were having a hay day. Ergo, Titus rose to the occasion to maintain solid teaching and oversight.

In an exhortation from one apostle (Paul) to another apostle (Titus), a strong reminder surfaces at the start of chapter 3 in the book about submission and obedience to various authorities within their communities.

Titus 3:3-7 reads,

"For we ourselves were also once foolish, disobedient, deceived, serving various lusts and pleasures, living in malice and envy, hateful, and hating one another. But when the **kindness** and the love of God our Savior toward man appeared, not by works of righteousness which we have done, but according to His mercy He saved us, through the washing of regeneration and renewing of the Holy Spirit, whom He poured out on us abundantly through Jesus Christ our Savior, that having been justified by His grace we should become heirs according to the hope of eternal life." (Emphasis mine)

Praise God that His kindness is instrumental in us becoming heavenly heirs who will inherit eternal life!

God's kindness, love, and mercy were at work through His beloved Son, Jesus Christ, even when we were foolish, disobedient, deceived, serving various lusts and pleasures, living in malice and envy, hateful, and hating one another. That's a powerful display of God's best when we're at our worst.

Also, God's kindness leads us to repentance according to Romans 2:4. (NIV)

"Or do you show contempt for the riches of his kindness, forbearance and patience, not realizing that God's kindness is intended to lead you to repentance?"

After we repent and accept Jesus Christ as our personal Lord and Savior, we're commanded to love our enemies, bless those who curse us, do good to those who hate us, and pray for those who spitefully use us and persecute us. (Matthew 5:44) That's a really tall order and entirely impossible to do in the flesh. To accomplish this, we need the Holy Spirit's help.

This is the reason I deem that kindness is a form of "spiritual currency" because this type of challenging kindness is the equivalent of something you can spend or distribute.

An act of kindness affects a person's heart and spirit in more ways than we can ever imagine.

I remember hearing a true story of one woman's kindness which transformed one man's life. She developed cancer and had to have reconstructive surgery which required many follow-up visits to this particular doctor's office.

The patient was quite timid by nature and in dire need of this man's God-given talents, especially since there were not many in this particular geographic area who possessed his abilities. The doctor had an extremely difficult personality and more earthly currency than he knew what to do with it.

As a result of many repetitive appointments, the doctor was totally befuddled because each time his patient was in his exam room, she exuded extreme kindness via the way she spoke (Proverbs 31:26) and conducted herself. The Greek word ***chrestotes*** was on classic display.

Plugging in Romans 2:4 above, this woman, operating by and through the riches of God's kindness, forbearance, and patience, overcame and subdued the priority of the man's physical riches. That's an awesome victory!

To hear the story, it's obvious that initially neither one of them probably tumbled to what was taking place, especially in the spiritual realm.

To make a short story long, the doctor eventually softened considerably, accepted Jesus Christ as his personal Lord and Savior, proposed to his patient, and the couple lived happily ever after. Isn't that an amazing story of the power of kindness that can be totally transformative?

Does kindness come naturally to you?

_____
_____
_____

If not, perhaps it's like everything else in life that requires cultivation and practice. It's never too late to start as eventually, it will become part of your lifestyle and overall witness to others in our world.

Prophetic Insights for Daily Living:

Thankfully, all of us are a spiritual work in progress. None of us is perfect as only Jesus Christ is. Kindness is one of the fruits of the Spirit mentioned in Galatians 5:22. If this is something with which you need help, pray and ask God to assist you with growth in this area.

There is an unexplainable spiritual principle that does take place when we genuinely choose, without ulterior motive, to do something kind for someone who's been extremely unkind to us. It's a "freeing" of sorts, kind of like when we choose to totally forgive someone who's done something horrible to us. Forgiveness sets us free and onto a path of healing even if the other person doesn't accept our forgiveness or has passed away, and there's no way to connect with him or her.

Proverbs 25:21-22 married up with Romans 12:20 presents powerful word pictures. Obviously, we wouldn't go around and heap coals of fire on the heads of our enemies! The spiritual lesson here speaks of believers who are free from malice, hate, and vengeance and have a merciful heart toward their enemies. Therefore, through random acts of kindness, believers in Jesus Christ help to lead them toward repentance. Quite often, physical acts of kindness are paired with spiritual acts of kindness such as praying for our enemies and witnessing to them about the truth of salvation and eternal life.

Seeking our own vengeance does not overcome evil. It usually results in each person trying to outdo the other in retaliating. Heaping burning coals on someone's head would be, in the physical realm, a way of inflicting pain and scarring on the person to avenge a wrong the person did.

We are not to seek vengeance against those who harm us, for we do not know whether they will repent before the second coming of the Lord. It is Jesus Who forgives sins, not us. It is also not up to us to avenge a wrong done to us. Rather, doing good to those who do evil to us is spiritually heaping coals of fire on their heads. (Romans 12:17-21; Hebrews 10:30-31; 2 Thessalonians 1:6-8)

So, even if we're short of physical cash this holiday season, we can still plan to lavishly spend spiritual kindness which is an invaluable currency!

https://sheilaeismann.com/christmas-themes/

Sheila Eismann, Prophetic Seer, Blogger, Author & Teacher, publishes her weekly blog posts endeavoring to encourage others through God's word. Her writings include teaching and instructions on how to apply prophetic insights for daily living. You can subscribe to receive new blog posts on her website at www.sheilaeismann.com.

Comfort at Christmas
December 23, 2020
Holidays

As we've been preparing for this upcoming holiday season, one of the many Christmas themes that has emerged is <u>**COMFORT @ CHRISTMAS**</u>. This has been reflected in gifts, cards, social media, recipes, special requests, holiday sales, and on rolls the proverbial river.

Each of us draws comfort from different people, things, situations, memories, pictures, or events.

The above items I've mentioned deal primarily with physical comfort; however, we must not overlook the all-important spiritual aspect since our bodies, souls, and spirits are all intricately connected. Drawing inspiration and strength from the Apostle Paul in the New Testament, his words from 2 Corinthians 1:3-5 seem most appropriate,

"Blessed *be* the God and Father of our Lord Jesus Christ, the Father of mercies and God of all comfort, who comforts us in all our tribulation, that we may be able to comfort those who are in any trouble, with the comfort with which we ourselves are comforted by God. For as the sufferings of Christ abound in us, so our consolation also abounds through Christ."

All of us have been challenged beyond our limits in many areas during this entire year as we've suffered the loss of loved ones, jobs, or businesses; had to remain flexible in virtually all areas of our lives, work from home, adapt to partial virtual learning for our children, cancel travel plans and some family gatherings and reunions; and the list seems to have no end.

Speaking of comfort at Christmas, I've been giving a lot of thought this week to the birth of our precious Lord and Savior, Jesus Christ.

Looking way back in time to approximately two millennia ago, Mary and Joseph's abode was part of the Roman Empire. Driven by a monetary motive, Caesar Augustus, the Roman Emperor, ordered a census to be taken of everyone within the region. Part of the edict ordered inhabitants to return to their place of origin and record their names there.

This required Joseph and Mary to travel about 70 miles from Nazareth to Bethlehem since Joseph's family hailed from that area, and he was of the house and lineage of David. The majority of the people walked; however, some people were fortunate enough to own a donkey to help them during this journey. Can you imagine the arduous trek for Mary using this mode of transportation just before Jesus' birth?

Due to the sudden, large influx of people arriving in Bethlehem to register for the mandated census, virtually every bed in each house was already taken. This resulted in Joseph and Mary having to stay at the Inn with the animals. It was customary to keep animals inside, especially at night, as they contributed to the overall warmth. The people would typically sleep on the upper level of the structure with the animals on the lower one. Since heat rises, this rendered extra comfort to those above.

It was in this setting that the Savior of the world safely arrived. Mary wrapped her beloved son in swaddling cloths and laid Him in the same manger in which the animals ate their food.

In my heart and spirit, I choose to believe that during this uncomfortable time, God comforted Joseph, Mary, and their newborn son as only He can do by and through the power of The Holy Spirit. Has God ever done something similar for you? If so, what was it, and how did He do it? It's definitely worth remembering even if He used unconventional methods and means.

_____
_____
_____
_____

At the time of Jesus' birth, a new, bright star appeared in the night sky. Reigning over Bethlehem of Judea in those days was none other than King Herod. Upon inquiry regarding the star from eastern wise men who traveled to Jerusalem, he ordered a search for the exact location of the Christ child to feign worship for Him.

Thank God for His timely, prophetic dreams! After visiting baby Jesus and His family, the wise men were divinely warned in a dream that they should not return to King Herod but travel back to their own country via a different route.

When he saw that he'd been outwitted, King Herod flew into a rage and issued a death edict for all male children under age two in Bethlehem and all its districts. This was a most unfortunate fulfillment of an Old Testament prophecy found in Jeremiah 31:15 and a classic display of the spirit of jealousy. King Herod was extremely jealous of and threatened by the birth of

Jesus. Suffice it to say, these types of "Christmas Themes" are not beneficial to anyone.

This demonic spirit of jealousy has many manifestations, chief among which are anger and murder. We find the original mention of this spirit in Numbers 5:14. Even though this is first listed in the Old Testament, it's obviously alive and well today, unfortunately.

Just as there was envy over Jesus' birth, this could happen to any of us as well. It pays to be aware of this element, so we can be prepared to deal with it.

https://sheilaeismann.com/dream-therapy/

There are some other aspects of Jesus' birth that are noteworthy. Were you fortunate enough to view the Christmas Star on the evening of December 21st which was also the Winter Solstice? In nothing less than a spectacular astronomical display, there was an exceptionally bright planetary conjunction of Jupiter and Saturn. They were lined up so close together that they appeared as one bright, shining star. Residents of planet earth had not been treated to something like this in the last 800 years, and it will not occur again until 2080. How many of us will still be alive by then?

As I've pondered this, what was downloaded to my spirit was this awesome, planetary event that could signal a new birth in our individual lives, the kingdom of God on earth, our nation, or other nations of the world.

Prophetic Insights for Daily Living:

1. What is God trying to birth in you?

_____
_____
_____
_____

2. It could be one of His Holy Spirit gifts listed in Romans 12:6-8 or 1 Corinthians 12:1-12 as well as Jesus' gifts to the church outlined in Ephesians 4:11-12.

3. Birthing can be messy, painful, but joyful.

4. We may not be able to discern the new thing that God is doing in our lives right away.

5. Isaiah 43:19 almost guarantees that we shall know it eventually when God does it.

6. Psalm 19:1- with the heavens declaring the glory of God and the firmament showing His handiwork, let's be sure to give Him praise in the newness of what He is doing.

Are you the type of person who likes to create Christmas themes?

_____
_____
_____
_____

If so, here's my Comfort at Christmas challenge or invitation:

Despite a tumultuous 2020, I would like to encourage you to give some thought as to how you might lend comfort to someone else. It could be something as small as a smile or a Secret Santa gift as extravagant as you want it to be. Creativity has no bounds, and it's more blessed to give than to receive. (Acts 20:35)

Speaking of gifts, the ones presented to Jesus at His birth were gold, frankincense, also known as olibanum, and myrrh. In ancient times, frankincense and myrrh were used in the holy incense burned in the temple.

The wise men chose these gifts because they were the ones customarily given to a king. It's interesting to note that they were presented to Jesus ahead of the fulfillment of his kingship.

Gold is symbolic of kingship or kingdom glory on earth. The Jews refused to acknowledge Jesus as king because they were incorrectly looking for a political one rather than a spiritual ruler or king.

Frankincense symbolizes fragrance, prayers, and intercession. The most important symbol is the deity. The battle still rages on earth over the deity of Jesus Christ even though He died over 1,900 years ago. This is where you can easily separate the true from the false, i.e., the true churches versus the cults. The latter claim and teach that Jesus' atoning death on the cross is insufficient for salvation alone. This explains why they add other works and traditions of men to their diabolical mixture. (Matthew 15:1-16; Mark 7:1-23)

If you are lashed up in one of these types of religious organizations, examine them closely and compare their doctrine to the actual Bible as opposed to their own version or translation thereof. If you find an error, depart while you still have time. (Ephesians 2:8-9; 1 John 2:2; Revelation 18:4)

Myrrh, an oil used in embalming, represents fragrance, suffering, and death. This was used for Jesus' burial. Before this, He was offered wine and myrrh at His crucifixion. (Mark 15:23) In John 19:39, we find the account of Joseph of Arimathea and Nicodemus bringing a 100-pound mixture in which to wrap Jesus' body.

What Christmas gift would you like to give to Jesus?

_____
_____
_____
_____

In times past, we've baked a birthday cake in honor of Him even though it's speculated that He wasn't actually born on Christmas but in the fall of the year. However, the important thing is that we celebrate Him and all that He's done for us and our families, especially dying on the cross for our sins, so that we can have eternal life. (2 Corinthians 5:21)

Merry Christmas to you and yours. If you're not already in the habit of doing so, perhaps you could add to your ongoing Christmas themes the reading of the Christmas Story found in Matthew 1-2 and Luke 1-2 as we continue to honor Jesus Christ, Who truly is the reason for the season.

Sheila Eismann, Prophetic Seer, Blogger, Author & Teacher, publishes her weekly blog posts endeavoring to encourage others through God's word. Her writings include teaching and instructions on how to apply prophetic insights for daily living. You can subscribe to receive new blog posts on her website at www.sheilaeismann.com.

Prophetic Dream: Rehashing The Past

December 30, 2020
Prophetic Dreams

Do you like hash? If so, what kind? Also, do you eat leftover hash? These may seem like peculiar questions to ask before launching my weekly blog post which is the last one for this year. While some people enjoy rehashing the past time and time again, is there really any benefit to doing so? Can a food analogy assist us with dream therapy and/or interpretation?

Early Sunday morning, December 20, 2020, and with 20 symbolizing redemption, so we have triple the amount, I had the following short, prophetic dream:

A man I know in real life called me on the phone. Even though I was in a deep sleep, I could hear the phone ring, and he immediately began to talk. I didn't even have time to say, "Hello."

There was a measure of background noise, and some of the time during the conversation, his voice faded in and out. However, I heard the repeated litany of what he was saying.

This man was very discontent and began to air the multitude of grievances during his life; how he thought he had been disenfranchised; other people had what should have been rightfully his and so forth.

In the first part of the conversation, he mentioned a woman named Cindy but did not state her last name.

The majority of the complaints pertained to this man's current place of employment, and he'd served in that general type of work for over three decades.

This dream lasted only about 5 minutes, and I never did speak in the dream. I only listened. Then I awakened suddenly.

End of dream.

Part of the clue to the dream could lie in the lifetime scripture verse which accompanies the name Cindy:

"Psalm 27:1, 'The Lord is my light and my salvation; whom shall I fear? The Lord is the stronghold of my life; of whom shall I be afraid?'" (KJV)

In real life, this man battled tremendous fear of man his whole adult life. The companion scripture verse for Cindy's name counters this. It asks the rhetorical question, "Whom shall I fear?"

The only fear we're to have is the holy, reverential fear of God. I delve into this in greater detail in Chapter 3 of my Bible Study titled *A Woman of Substance*.

https://sheilaeismann.com/product/a-woman-of-substance/

Psalm 27 also instructs us that the Lord is to be the stronghold of our life. Just as with so many other things, there are beneficial strongholds and negative ones. Fear of man would be a stellar example of the latter.

According to Proverbs 29:25, "The fear of man brings a snare, but whoever trusts in the LORD shall be safe."

Safe from what? Obviously, safe from whatever is in the trap which is just waiting to ensnare us.

Other relevant scriptures are Deuteronomy 1:17; 1 Samuel 15:24; Isaiah 51:12; Luke 12:4; John 9:22, 19:38; and Galatians 2:12.

The man in the dream was a slave to other people's opinions and continually asked, "What did thus and such person say about me recently?"

He had a strong evangelistic anointing which he never submitted to, accepted, and allowed The Holy Spirit to develop within him. (Ephesians 4:11-12)

He was not content with the destiny that God chose for him nor did he accept God's will for his life.

Psalm 37:3-5 is most instructive, but our flesh screams loudly and rails against this some of the time:

"Trust in the Lord, and do good;
Dwell in the land, and feed on His faithfulness.
Delight yourself also in the Lord,
And He shall give you the desires of your heart.

Commit your way to the Lord,
Trust also in Him,
And He shall bring *it* to pass."

Why is this so difficult? How often do we want to **fully** submit our will to God's will, so He will give us the desire of our hearts? There are times when we want to stay in the driver's seat instead of the passenger one.

Back to the man featured in the dream for a moment. What's so sad is that he actually achieved a great deal in his life, but it was as if he was looking for success in all the wrong places and was perpetually discontent instead of being content with who God created him to be. With contentment is great gain. (1 Timothy 6:6)

What's ironic is this man in the dream who called me on the phone actually thought in real life that he should have been given the opportunities, positions, etc. that another man I know in real life was actually given.

Sometimes in the prophetic, we can find ourselves "in the middle," so to speak, as we will sort of know both sides of the equation. This means that we need to increase our intercessory prayer for all involved, not just one party.

Also, throughout the course of his life, the man in the dream had a huge father wound from his earthly father. When this happens in our lives, it's important to submit to God as our Heavenly Father, so He can heal all our wounds by and through the power of The Holy Spirit.

None of us is a perfect parent by any stretch of the imagination, and it's impossible to go through life without suffering some kind of wound. In addition, we must extend grace since wounded people sometimes wound other people in turn until they learn how to not operate in that manner.

It's an exercise in futility for any one of us to continue to sit around and lick our wounds. The Apostle Paul had some great advice from his own life in this regard which we find in Philippians 3:13-14, "Brethren, I do not count myself to have apprehended; but one thing *I do,* forgetting those things which are behind and reaching forward to those things which are ahead, I press toward the goal for the prize of the upward call of God in Christ Jesus."

Therefore, in reviewing this dream, it's important to notice the following demonic spirits having a hay day:

spirit of bondage – Romans 8:15

spirit of fear – 2 Timothy 1:7

spirit of jealousy – Numbers 5:14

spirit of heaviness – Isaiah 61:3

We can recognize what's going on in our lives by the daily fruit that is revealed. The difference is listed in Galatians 5:22-23. The Holy Spirit will help us grow His fruit within us if we will just give Him full permission and cooperate with Him.

Since this dream was given to me on the 20th with the triple theme of redemption, I'm praying for this man who called me and others who may be struggling with not accepting themselves for who God intended them to be. It's sad when someone desires to be someone else or wants another person's life instead of his or her own. God created us to be just who we are. If He would have wanted us to be someone else, He definitely had the power to do just that!

There's a little song we used to teach the kiddos at Vacation Bible School. One of the lines was, "Thank you, Father, for making me me!" That still resides within my heart.

20 also represents responsibility and accountability. Maturity in Christ our Lord requires that we grow up in Him. (1 Corinthians 13:11; Ephesians 3:17-19, 4:15; and 2 Peter 3:18)

God reveals His will and assignments, in part, through prophetic dreams and visions. This dream is an intercessory prayer assignment for me.

Prophetic Insights for Daily Living:

1. What have been some of your intercessory prayer assignments from God?

_____
_____
_____
_____

2. In what manner or method did you receive them?

_____
_____
_____
_____

3. What was the final outcome or answer?

_____
_____

4. How did you grow or what did you learn throughout the process?

5. Do you enjoy praying for others, different geographic regions, real difficult dilemmas or situations, injustices, unsaved people, etc.?

6. There's always so much to pray about. Perhaps this is one reason we may be given different assignments or burdens.

7. Do you have any suggestions as to how I can be praying for the man in the dream?

8. Here's sort of a humorous yet direct application for this blog post if you're interested:

Locate a hash recipe that looks good if you don't already have one in your midst, triple it, and eat it for several days straight. At the end of about day 10, how does it taste? How could this apply to rehashing our past?

Just for grins, and to continue to celebrate the holidays, you might enjoy making this Red Flannel Hash. Try it. You'll like it! Some people attest to the fact that cooking is a type of therapy in and of itself. It might even be a first cousin to dream therapy.

https://www.simplyrecipes.com/recipes/red_flannel_hash/

As we close out 2020 with its symbolism, may this catapult us into 2021 as we marry it up with the meaning for 21 which is fullness or completion, the expectancy of God as to what He's going to do, and serving Him.

Happy New Year, and all the best to you in 2021!

Sheila Eismann, Prophetic Seer, Blogger, Author & Teacher, publishes her weekly blog posts endeavoring to encourage others through God's word. Her writings include teaching and instructions on how to apply prophetic insights for daily living. You can subscribe to receive new blog posts on her website at www.sheilaeismann.com.

Sheila Eismann, Idaho native, author, and publisher of 15 books was raised on Sage Creek Farms in Southwestern Idaho. She pens inspirational and fictional books drawing upon her life experiences as a legal secretary, law firm office administrator, office manager for a national horse breed registry, and successful operator of a bookkeeping business. Midway through life, she discovered published authors and poets on both sides of her family. Eismann, a co-founder of ICAN (Idaho Creative Author's Network), speaks at Writer's and Women's Conferences. She endeavors to be an encourager with a sense of humor. Learn more about Sheila, read her weekly blog posts, and discover her books at **www.sheilaeismann.com**.

Where to find Sheila Eismann online:

Email: sheila@sheilaeismann.com

Website: www.sheilaeismann.com

Facebook: www.facebook.com/sheila.eismann

Blog: www.sheilaeismann.com

LinkedIn: Sheila Eismann

Sheila's and Dan's books are also featured online in Sheila's Etsy shop: www.etsy.com/shop/BooksbySheilaEismann

Sheila invites you to check out her new website **www.sheilaeismann.com** and sign up to receive her blog posts in your email inbox. Please send her an email at **sheila@sheilaeismann.com** to say hello and to let her know what ministered to you the most in this workbook or your favorite blog post. Happy reading and studying!

OTHER BOOKS AVAILABLE FROM AUTHORS SHEILA EISMANN, DAN EISMANN & DESERT SAGE PRESS which can be purchased from: www.sheilaeismann.com or www.amazon.com.

Read and study with **Sheila Eismann,** Prophetic Author, Blogger, Speaker, and Teacher, in Volume 2 of her latest series titled *Prophetic Insights for Daily Living.* This **233-page** workbook can be used as a stand-alone devotional, individual Bible Study, or in a group study. Sheila describes various dreams, visions, prophetic words, and teachings she's been given by The Holy Spirit from January 2021 through May 2021 which are designed to help you grow in spiritual knowledge and the operation of The Holy Spirit gifts. Each entry includes questions, contemplation, reflection, or a call to action.

Western Fiction Book One of The Sabblonti Series, *Jantzi's Jokers*, features Jantzi Belle, the matriarch of the Sabblonti family, who has worked for decades to keep her cattle empire intact. Life takes a drastic turn when she receives a late-night visitor. The brief disappearance of her Last Will and Testament could complicate matters between her daughters, Stormy and Sarita. Stormy and her husband, Chet Castins, are struggling to work through the loss of their three children. Against all odds, drifter Wyn Moreland makes a bold move when he decides that Sarita is his beauty to rescue. The county veterinarian, Dr. Ben Shaw, is also vying for her affections. Will Wyn emerge as the winner? Just before the dawn of the New Year, revelations come forth regarding forgery, cattle rustling, and land exploitation. Will the Sabblonti Empire survive, and more importantly, who will control its reins?

The Sabblonti Saga accelerates in Book Two of the Series, **A Stormy Year**. Riding her high horse after inheriting the family fortune, Stormy Castins is determined to reinvent herself following her husband's accident. Blinded by jealousy, ambition, and naivety, she hires Less and Meg Alotto to oversee her vast high desert mountain domain. While Stormy is away, the cattle herd ends up in disarray.

Amidst the hot dry season, romance is blooming on several fronts despite a major showdown during a mid-summer celebration. The pesky Black Raven continues to wreak havoc at the most inopportune times.

Unable to overcome the vengeance which strikes by way of a mysterious range fire combined with the dire deeds of a cagey couple, the Sabblonti Ranch is in shambles just as Stormy starts to regain her senses. Humility is the prescription needed to open her eyes to realize what's truly important in life. The sparks from a belated holiday Rendevous set Chet and Stormy on their path to recovery.

Desperation explodes when heiress Stormy Sabblonti Castins calculates her dwindling fortune in Book 3 of the Sabblonti Series, **Love the Tie that Binds.** Is she capable of learning the painful lessons of having to rely upon someone and something other than inherited wealth? As her husband, Chet continues to heal from his near-fatal accident, tormenting shadows of The Black Raven lurk in the background.

These high desert hills are alive with blessed babies, enchanting engagements, skillful scavengers, sophisticated scoundrels, rich revelations, timeless treasures, and western weddings.

The Main Sabblonti Ranch house abounds with an unexpected marriage, childrens' voices, and Sir Shelton sporting his silver bell.

In a captivating story of courage, trust, and faithfulness, will Stormy still be tied in knots or find lasting love by the year's end?

Share the joys and sorrows of a mountain community in this swirling saga.

In this collection of true stories titled ***Stirrings of The Spirit***, author Sheila Eismann invites you to walk with her family through several valleys en route to some mountain tops as they learned to rely on God in the most harrowing of circumstances.

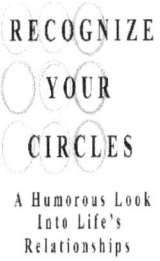

Have you ever wondered why you were the last one to hear of THE big social event of the year? Well, wonder no longer after reading this e-book titled ***Recognize Your Circles***! When volunteering for an organization years ago, author Sheila Eismann was introduced to the concept of "the circles of your life." Since the idea was so beneficial to her, she decided to share it with all of you.

Straight from the Horse's Trough is a humorous read to assist the suburbanite or urbanite who desires to live a healthier lifestyle by growing his or her own food, but is faced with the challenge of a small space in which to do so. This e-book is chock full of how-to steps and includes pictures to remove the guesswork from the project.

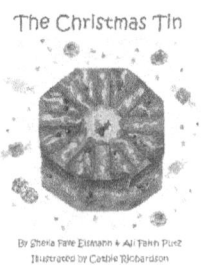

The Christmas Tin is a most delightful read for the young at heart anytime during the year. This endearing book is based upon a true story featuring the older of the two authors when she was a young girl and conveys the timeless message that "love truly is the best gift of all." Children will especially enjoy all of the colorful illustrations contained within this treasure. There's a sugar cookie recipe included in the book and a helpful holiday suggestion for the kiddos to bless someone who's not expecting it at all!

Freedom is Your Destiny! Vietnam Veteran, Dan Eismann, using combat experiences to illustrate spiritual truths, invites you to take a journey with him as he presents a rock-solid strategy for not only fighting your spiritual battles but winning the all-important war. In the midst thereof, the most vital aspect is realizing you can experience freedom and become all that God has destined you to be!

Settle into your special reading spot; grab a cup of tea or your favorite meal. Be stirred as you read and ponder **Poetry Time, Volume One**; allow Sheila's words to encourage and heal.

Everyone can use a little encouragement ~~ a dose of what is beneficial, ethical, and honorable. **Heart to Heart From God's Word** provides this for you. Penned with humor and wisdom, the daily tidbits are paired with Bible verses that convey life-changing principles which are designed for readers of all ages transcending cultures and continents. This devotional will challenge you to grow and fulfill your God-given destiny. It can also double as a prayer journal.

A Woman of Substance is a practical, interactive, and entertaining 12-week Bible study penned to help equip you to fulfill your God-given destiny and impact the culture for Jesus Christ at the same time. It can be used as a stand-alone study or devotional and works well in a group setting, too. It is designed for women ages junior high through adult.

ADDITIONAL NOTES & REFLECTIONS

ADDITIONAL NOTES & REFLECTIONS

ADDITIONAL NOTES & REFLECTIONS

ADDITIONAL NOTES & REFLECTIONS

ADDITIONAL NOTES & REFLECTIONS

ADDITIONAL NOTES & REFLECTIONS

ADDITIONAL NOTES & REFLECTIONS

ADDITIONAL NOTES & REFLECTIONS

ADDITIONAL NOTES & REFLECTIONS

ADDITIONAL NOTES & REFLECTIONS

ADDITIONAL NOTES & REFLECTIONS

ADDITIONAL NOTES & REFLECTIONS

ADDITIONAL NOTES & REFLECTIONS

[i] Keesee, Ruby, Bible Studies for Women: The Gift of the Word of Knowledge (Caldwell, Idaho, 1990), PP. 1-4.

Keesee, Ruby, Bible Studies for Women: The Gift of the Word of Wisdom (Caldwell, Idaho, 1990), PP. 1-2.

[ii] Keesee, Ruby, Bible Studies for Women: The Gift of Discerning of Spirits, (Caldwell, Idaho, 1990), PP. 1-4.

[iii] Jeremiah 23:28.

[iv] AMG Dictionary – Old Testament, word 5030.

[v] Deuteronomy 18:18.

[vi] Jeremiah 20:8.

[vii] Jeremiah 20:9.

[viii] AMG Dictionary – Old Testament, word 2374.

[ix] AMG Dictionary – Old Testament, word 7200.

[x] Jeremiah 1:7, 9, 11, 12.

[xi] 1 Chronicles 29:29–30.

[xii] 2 Samuel 12:1–4.

[xiii] 2 Samuel 12:5.

[xiv] 2 Samuel 11:2–12:9.

[xv] Luke 1:5, 7, 11, 13, 16–17.

[xvi] 2 Chronicles 24:18–19.

[xvii] Acts 11:27–30.

[xviii] Acts 15:32.

[xix] Acts 13:1–3.

[xx] Jeremiah 1:9–10.

[xxi] House, Paul R. (2008) Note to Jeremiah 1:10. L. T. Dennis (Ex. Ed.), ESV Study Bible, English Standard Version. Wheaton, Ill.: Crossway Bibles.

[xxii] 1 Thessalonians 5:20–21.

[xxiii] 1 Corinthians 14:29–32.

[xxiv] Luke 2:36; Acts 2:17; 21:6.

www.ingramcontent.com/pod-product-compliance
Lightning Source LLC
Chambersburg PA
CBHW080637170426
43200CB00015B/2875